THE YIN AND YANG OF BUSINESS COMMUNICATION

THE YIN AND YANG OF BUSINESS COMMUNICATION

Laurel Alexander

2000

First published in 2002 by Management Books 2000 Ltd
Forge House, Limes Road
Kemble, Cirencester
Gloucestershire, GL7 6AD, UK
Tel: 0044 (0) 1285 771441/2
Fax: 0044 (0) 1285 771055
E-mail: m.b.2000@virgin.net
Web: mb2000.com

Printed and bound in Great Britain by Biddles, Guildford

British Library Cataloguing in Publication Data is available

ISBN 1-85252-389-1

Contents

‘On the one hand, we’ll never experience childbirth. On the other hand, we can all open our own jars.’

Bruce Willis, on the difference between men and women

Preface

The three key areas I believe that make a business profitable (and therefore successful) are marketing know-how, financial acumen and people skills.

No matter how brilliant your idea, how marvellous your marketing strategy or how ingeniously you balance your cash flow, if you can't relate effectively to work colleagues, employees and your customers or clients, business could go pear-shaped. Granted, we don't need to win a personality contest at work, but we do need interpersonal skills, which will enable us to do the job productively, enable us to persuade other people to do their job productively and to make sales.

If we are in the business of business, we need interpersonal skills so that we understand what makes people tick and how to work alongside them for the mutual benefit of a win-win situation.

This is a book written for anyone in business who wants to communicate better with the opposite gender and is about understanding the differences in communication styles and working with those differences for the improvement of the business.

NOTE: Throughout the book, there are many examples of how men communicate and how women communicate. These are general examples and there are exceptions to the rule with both genders.

Laurel Alexander
laurelalexander@pavilion.co.uk

Introduction to Yin and Yang

One of the best-known symbols in Chinese Philosophy is the T'ai Chi Chu symbol, the circular symbol representing the concept of yin and yang. Although it traces its origins to ancient Chinese cosmology, it gained its philosophical sense in the 4th century B.C. The philosophy of Yin and Yang is said to date back nearly 6,000 years to the third or fourth millennium B.C. and is attributed to an enlightened philosopher named Fu Shi (also credited with creating the I-Ching or Book of Changes). The basic premise of yin and yang is the notion that the only constant factor in natural phenomena is universal change. In other words, nothing remains the same; no disease, no condition, no emotion, no treatment or diagnosis, absolutely everything is in a constant state of flux and, therefore, subject to the laws of change.

The image of yin and yang is a circle, half black and half white, each half invading the other's hemisphere. Inside each drop is a dot of the opposite colour. This swirl represents the endless cycling process of life. In Taoism, life is seen as a full circle rather than a pinnacle to be achieved. Literally meaning the 'dark' and 'sunny' sides of a hill, yin and yang represent the contrasting sides of nature e.g. good/evil, active/passive, positive/negative, light/dark, summer/winter, male/female.

Although yin and yang are in tension, they are not in opposition to each other. There is, for example, no definite male and female, as each contains part of the other. They are mutually dependent partners and neither can exist without the other. They complement and balance one another in an endless cycle.

It is important to remember that yin and yang are not static concepts and that they are constantly influencing and determining one another. There is always some measure of yin within yang and vice versa. To use the analogy of a hillside; during the day the sunlit side of the hill is yang within yang, while the shaded side is yin within yang. Conversely, at night the moonlit side of the hill is yang within yin while the dark side of the hill is yin within yin. In this fluid model, it must be understood that neither yin nor yang can ever exist without the other.

Yin (female)

The female principle of yin is associated with that which maintains and endures, it is nourishing and supports growth and development as well as being something contracting and moving inward.

Yang (male)

Yang is that which is creative and generating, it develops and expands; it is dynamic and full of movement.

Part 1

The Differences of Gender

Valuing Diversity

The Role of Gender in Business

Management, Leadership and Gender

The Differences of Gender

Gender differences in values

Four major areas of research highlight male-female differences in dominance or striving for superiority (and the inevitable feelings of success or failure).

1. Key research shows how women's values differ from men's. Women are concerned with developing personal relationships and helping others; men compete for powerful positions.
2. Developmental psychology shows boys' aggressiveness and resistance to control by females.
3. Linguistics shows how women's fundamental purpose is different from men's when they converse. Men are always 'proving themselves'; women are always trying to be liked.
4. Research in learning shows that women attempt to learn in different ways from men. Women try to identify with the person expressing a different opinion so they can see the reasoning and new perspective involved; men almost immediately start to question and argue with the different view.

Men become much more involved than women in intellectually figuring out what is fair and what are individual rights, such as in making rules, e.g. in religion, and the family and laws, e.g. in politics. For men, differences of opinion tend to be worked out via logical arguments and courts of law; for women, differences tend to be worked out by talking to each other, considering each other's viewpoints, and understanding each other's needs. Men are more concerned with becoming independent, being free to do their own thing, and being as successful as they can be. Women tend to be more concerned with fulfilling their responsibilities to others than with assuring their own rights; more involved with building caring relationships than 'breaking away' to make their own way; more into helping others than getting ahead themselves.

Keep in mind that boys must gain their masculine identification by separating from mother, while girls attach and take on the characteristics of mother. Thus, for this reason and others, males may tend to see danger in connecting with others – in getting too close or too dependent on someone or in confronting someone. Doing battle in court is more a man's style. Females may see danger in disconnecting with others – in loneliness or successful advancement or rejection. Intimacy is scary to males but a source of security to females. Autonomy is scary to females but a source of pride to males. To males, human relationships are seen as a hierarchy based on power and status; they want to climb to the top and feel afraid if others get too close to them. For most men, achievement takes priority over intimacy until mid-life when suddenly males realise what they have been missing.

Males identify themselves and their success by their accomplishments; females identify themselves by their relationships. To females, relationships are more like a network of safety and care among equals; they want to be in the centre of the network and fear getting too far out on the edge. Women recognise more openly their interdependence on others and see the powerful person as being able and willing to help and nurture others. Men see power as the ability to control others. To males, 'being responsible' in a relationship means not doing what you want to do out of consideration of others. To females, 'being responsible' means doing what others are counting on you to do, regardless of what you want to do.

Justice tells us that everyone should be treated the same; personal caring tells us to do more than just not hurt anyone – we must help everyone who needs it. Women, giving us a different moral perspective from males, can help all of us be more caring, more responsible, and less aggressive. Thus, we all need to 'learn to think like a woman' as well as like a man. Think of the changes that might occur if world leaders were committed to justice and to responsible caring, rather than just to defending our rights and possessions with weapons.

Anger vs. tears

It is socially more acceptable for men to show anger and aggression, whereas it is not socially acceptable for women to show anger and aggression. I've heard it said that in the workplace, when a man loses his temper and yells, it's viewed as taking control. When a woman loses her temper and yells, it's viewed as losing control. Same behaviour, totally disparate perceptions due solely to gender differences.

Society establishes gender roles for us

The different ways of males and females interacting fit nicely with differences in men's and women's value systems. Women value being sensitive and maintaining good relationships, e.g. attachment over achievement; men value gaining status by following 'the rules', e.g. achievement over attachment. Since our society values competition and individuals being successful on their own, women's orientation towards caring for others and/or cooperatively building the community is considered (by the male dominated society) to be of lesser importance. These value differences are reflected in the gender roles established by our culture, such as:

- Males are urged to excel, e.g. to become the MD – they are supposed to grow up to be powerful; they don't show their weaknesses; they are valued; they are preferred; they are encouraged more and prepared better for careers than females are; they are expected to be tough, independent, demanding, aggressive, good problem-solvers, and on and on. Thus, men are expected and prepared to strive for superiority. In short, the rules for men are:
    1. Don't be a sissy (no whining)
    2. Be important (be superior to others)
    3. Be tough (be self-sufficient)
    4. Be powerful (be strong and dominate others)
- Within the two-career families of today, the archaic sex role expectations are still subtly there. Our culture continues to

> pressure us to conform to these gender roles and do what we are supposed to do; the cultural, family, and friends' expectations become internalised as our own self-expectations; guilt may result if we don't follow the prescribed roles. Notice how people react to a man who decides to stay home and take care of the kids.

Gender roles limit what both males and females can do. In effect, these sex roles encourage us to be what others want us to be. We could be free to choose our own life goals and roles (from both male and female gender roles) and that is called androgyny (see Cook (1985), Bem (1976, 1993), Kaplan and Bem (1976), or Lorber (1994) for a discussion of gender roles and inequality). The most recent suggestion is to completely disassociate gender from all personality traits. Why should submissiveness or cooperation be considered feminine? They are *human* traits, not just traits of women! Just define what each personal trait, such as submissiveness, involves in terms of actions and feelings – and let each human being decide how submissive or cooperative he/she is and wants to be. Indeed, the current masculine-or-feminine classification of traits is silly, e.g. men are unemotional, women are illogical, men are independent, women are home-oriented, men are not concerned about their appearance, etc.

Competition vs. cooperation

Over and over it appears as though we are thinking about 'Who is on top?' and 'How do I measure up?' This destructive, competitive, win-lose situation, discussed fully by Kohn (1986), is connected with personally feeling superior, chauvinistic, or inferior to others. It takes Kohn an entire book to summarise the massive data indicating that competition in our society is harmful. Yet, our culture proclaims just the opposite, that competition is efficient, healthy, and fun. Actually, hard research indicates that people achieve more if they work cooperatively with others than if they work competitively. On the other hand, we can readily accept that a competitive job, where someone wins by making others fail, causes stress, resentment of the winner, contempt for the losers, low self-esteem, and major barriers to supportive relationships. What is the solution?

Kohn recommends replacing competition with cooperation, e.g. working together, assuming responsibility for helping each other do our best, and uncritically valuing each other's contributions. To change our goals in life from competition to cooperation, we need new values and a new philosophy of life. Competition implies a hierarchy; cooperation implies equality.

According to the sociolinguist and author, Deborah Tannen, women approach the world as individuals in a network of interpersonal connections, where everyone seeks to establish community, to eschew giving the impression of superiority and to support each other. The aim of communication is to create and maintain relationships and to avoid isolation. Women want to reach consensus and get, as well as give, support and confirmation in a conversation. In a talk, women therefore concentrate on whether the interlocutor remains aloof or tries to get closer. Men, on the other hand, look upon the world as hierarchically structured where it counts to achieve and maintain a high status, to stand up against other people and to preserve independence. For men, conversations are part of this struggle for a good social position, and so communication serves them as a means to gain and keep the upper hand and to challenge others. In a conversation, they rather focus on whether the interlocutor possibly tries to outdo, belittle or patronise them (Tannen, 1992).

Tannen mentions that women are of course also interested in achieving a high status and want to avoid being defeated, but they do not give it special emphasis; similarly, men want to preserve intimacy and avoid isolation too, but it is less important for them. She adds that women tend to pursue such 'male' goals ‘in the guise of connection’ and that men tend to pursue such female goals ‘in the guise of opposition’ (Tannen, 1992).

Independence vs. consensus

Men are more programmed for independence and superiority (due to past duties of hunting, protecting, etc.). On the other hand, responsible for relationships and considered less important than males, women are programmed more so for consensus and inferiority.

Identity

Men and women are often socialised in two different cultures. In each culture, they learn rules about how to identify self and how to go about influencing others. Extensive research over the past twenty years has found that men and women are more alike than different in personality characteristics, e.g. independence and dependence, and individual abilities, e.g. mathematical skills and verbal skills. But there are two key differences:

1. how we establish our identity and go about claiming who we are
2. how we go about influencing others' behaviours.

Women tend to establish their identity towards achieving social cohesion through affirmation of and cooperation with others. Men often establish identity through competition and dominance. One observable outcome to these two perspectives is that women will often blame themselves when something goes wrong, and men will often blame others when something goes wrong. Men often times go about influencing others' behaviours by using direct commands, whereas women will ask or request an action or behaviour.

Male logic and women's intuition

The split in our thinking between 'masculine' and 'feminine' is probably as old as language itself. Human beings seem to have a natural tendency to divide things into pairs: good/bad, light/dark, subject/object and so on. It is not surprising, then, that the male/female or masculine/feminine dichotomy is used to classify things other than men and women.

The association of Reason with men and Nature with women is well known, and has been widely criticised. Aristotle defined man as a 'rational animal', and by that he really meant men, not human beings. Unlike Plato, he saw women as less able to reason, hence less 'human' and more 'animal'. In Europe, well into the twentieth century, women were generally seen as somehow intellectually deficient.

Nearly all societies, from hunting and gathering tribes to post-industrial nations, offer some kind of compensation to those who lose out in the status game. For example, among the practically matriarchal Zuni Indians of New Mexico, the economically powerless men were credited with the ability to make rain. In the same way, women are compensated for their supposed inability to think rationally by women's intuition. Attempts were made to justify this in biological terms; women were seen as naturally more emotional and/or in touch with Nature because of their strange biology (menstruation, hormones). This was about as scientific as the Zuni Indians' theory that men could make rain.

Men and women are, of course, biologically different. There are even significant differences in male and female brains; women, for example, have a thicker corpus callosum (the thing that connects the two halves of the brain). However, it is a giant leap from observing that there are neurological differences between the sexes to assuming that these differences correspond to the classic Reason/Nature or logic/emotion dichotomies. In fact, some of these differences may even indicate the opposite. The left hemisphere of the brain generally deals with linear processing, as found in language and some types of mathematics, and this hemisphere develops faster in girls than in boys. The old 11-plus test of verbal reasoning used in British schools was actually adjusted to bring boys' scores up to the level of girls'!

Bonding styles

Men bond through tasks and activities, e.g. working on the car, playing sports. Women bond through talking.

Women readers: your partner comes in from a game of football. You ask him how the game was. 'Fine.' Then you ask what he and his friends talked about. 'Nothing.' He's serious! And if they did talk about something at any length, he doesn't remember what! Even so, he feels just as close to his friends as you do to yours; it's just a different style of bonding. Neither of these styles is right or wrong, good or bad, just different. Of course men do talk, but generally not to the degree women do and usually about sports, hobbies, or business - or women.

Women's conversation tends to emphasise feelings more, which may also mean that they think about feelings more. It does not, however, mean that women are more emotional. It is perfectly possible that men are just as emotional, but for social reasons they talk (and think) about their feelings less. Similarly, the fact that in most cultures men argue more about abstract things, does not mean that men are naturally more logical, it just means that the things men prefer to talk about require logical argument more than they require expression of feelings.

Logic is a set of principles for getting from something we already knew, to something we didn't. If we know that all horses eat grass, and we know that Neddy is a horse, we can use very simple logic to say that Neddy eats grass, even if we have never seen him eat anything. The more complex logic that we use in constructing philosophical arguments or designing computers is really only doing the same kind of thing.

Intuition is a trickier concept. We usually say that we arrive at an idea or solution to a problem intuitively when we know something without knowing how we came to know it. A scientist may arrive at a new theory because the idea just pops into his or her head, or even turns up in a dream. You may get an intuitive feeling that a person is dishonest without actually having heard him or her say something you know to be untrue. In both these cases, what seems to be happening is that the mind stores and sorts information unconsciously, providing us only with the end result of this process. There is no guarantee, of course, that this conclusion will be true; scientists would still have to perform experiments to prove their intuitive theories, and you would probably want some hard evidence to prove that the person you feel is dishonest really does tell lies.

There is therefore nothing particularly strange or mystical about intuition; it is something we do all the time. Why, then, do we talk about women's intuition, as though men never arrive at a conclusion without consciously following all the stages that were necessary to reach it? The answer is probably linguistic. As we have seen, traditionally women's conversation is less formal, less argumentative, and more concerned with feelings than men's conversation. Intuitive conclusions are therefore more acceptable in an all-female group. Men, on the other hand, are expected to argue more, and to argue more logically, presenting evidence in a systematic way to back up their conclusions.

Stress: withdraw vs. talk

Men tend to withdraw under stress. Remember, they were programmed for independence and superiority, and feel they should solve their own problems. If you have read *Men are from Mars, Women are from Venus*, John Gray tells us that men go into their caves when stressed. They don't want help; they want to figure it out themselves. So they go off some place where they can ponder the issue alone and process it. On the opposite end of the spectrum, women talk under stress for two reasons: they bond through sharing feelings and problems, and they are more verbal, so talking through issues helps them process and understand. What happens? Men see and hear women talking about all these problems and think, 'Good grief, she's going to have a nervous breakdown any second now!" No, it's just a style difference!

We can see, then, that logic and intuition are not only false, but also damaging, particularly to women. The fact that men often use logic, or at least logical-sounding arguments, to 'put women in their place' is not a fault of logic; it is the fault of those men's sexism and lack of social skills. More innocently, men are often accused of being cold and logical, not because there is anything wrong with their ideas, but because they do not understand the unspoken rules of female conversation, in the same way that women are often accused of being illogical or emotional because they do not argue using the same language as men.

If women reject logic and rely solely on feelings, they are left in the weak position of having to argue with feelings. Feeling that something is true does not make it true, and it will not convince anyone else that it is true either. You can say, 'I feel X", but the person you are arguing with can just as well reply, 'Well I don't." The result is that the argument usually goes nowhere. This is particularly damaging in arguments between men and women, since both sides are likely to go away with their prejudices strengthened; the men think women are subjective, emotional and illogical, and the women think men are impersonal, cold and over-intellectual. To justify their feelings of hurt at being beaten in an argument, the women concerned may go further and dismiss the whole thing as male logic, as though there were two types of logic, on for men and another for women. This then places the men in an impossible position, since if they attempt to be reasonable, they are accused again of using male logic, in the same way that if a woman gets upset in an argument, it is taken as proof that she is overly emotional, and hence irrational. This does not only lead to a lack of communication between the sexes, it leads to a lack of communication in which women come off worse, since policy is generally made as the result of argument, not sharing feelings.

Competition vs. harmony

Again because of leadership and protection responsibilities, men are programmed more for status and competition than women, whereas women are wired more for connection and harmony. Even in conversation these differences are demonstrated. According to Deborah Tannen, author of You Just Don't Understand: Women and Men In Conversation (William Morrow, 1990), men often view conversations as 'negotiations' in which they try to achieve status and maintain independence. Women, on the other hand, tend to see conversation as a way to connect with other people. Men prefer to be respected and admired; women prefer to be liked and approved of (I am not saying women don't want to be respected and admired, or men don't want to be liked.)

Behavioural styles

I have used the labels 'masculine' and 'feminine' here rather than 'male' and 'female' – all people have a combination of both behavioural styles. Understanding these differences, whether with a woman using a masculine style, a man with a feminine style, a woman with a feminine style, etc., will help you improve the productivity and effectiveness of your communication. Men and women have different styles of communicating and different requirements for communication. Women have traditionally been good listeners but have not focused on the attitudes of the speaker to gain advantage in negotiations. Maybe women need to learn to pick up on male clues by negotiating from a basis of strength. Learned behaviour styles include:

Masculine

- Independence
- Superiority
- Status
- Competition
- Being respected, admired
- Withdrawing under stress
- Bonding through talks and activities
- Allowing anger and aggression
- Not allowing tears, fear, confusion, etc.

- Difficulty in asking for help
- Handling conflict directly
- Speaking briefly and to the point

Feminine

- Consensus
- Inferiority; equality at best
- Connection
- Harmony
- Being liked, approved of
- Talking under stress
- Bonding through feelings and problems
- Allowing tears, fear, confusion, tenderness
- Not allowing anger, aggression
- Asking for help
- Avoiding fear, conflict
- Discussing things in detail

The woman, craving closeness and intimacy with her man, talks to him about her problems with friends, family, her job, etc. She seeks to have her man respond as her girlfriends have always done, and talk with her about his concerns. The man, however, hears these conversations as requests for advice, not intimacy. He considers the problem and offers a solution, or dismisses the issue, as the boys he knew always did. When his woman continues to go on about these same concerns, showing no movement to consider his advice, he becomes confused and eventually angry; he begins to believe that his woman is an expert at talking about nothing. The woman begins to feel that her man doesn't care about her because he won't talk to her in a way that feels intimate. It is important for women to understand that men's communicating is all about status.

The prime goal of males is to be able to mate and to do this they must be powerful enough to challenge the lead males in the herd. As they grow up, they bide their time by establishing a pecking order. When a male is big and strong enough to have most of the other males 'under' him, he is ready to take on the 'old man'. If he wins the fight, he gets to mate with the females of his choice (and they will mate only with him).

Tannen has found that human males behave in exactly the same way. She discussed the research of Marjorie Goodwin, who studied boys in Philadelphia for a year and a half. 'She found that boys give orders as a way of gaining social status. The high-status boys gave orders just to maintain their dominance, not because they particularly needed the thing done. And the boys who were being told what to do were low status, by virtue of doing what they were told.'

This dynamic is important to remember when looking at another major area of miscommunication between men and women. Women cannot understand the resistance men seem to have when asked for assistance or consideration of some kind or another. Women must remember the above scenario and understand that, for men, doing what they're asked to do means they have lost status in that relationship. Men often feel that women are trying to manipulate them. What a woman might see as a simple request is seen by her man an attempt to manipulate him into a 'one-down' position. Tannen discusses this issue further: 'Women want men to do what we want. We want them to want to do what we want, because that's what we do. If a woman perceives that something she's doing is really hurting a man, she wants to stop doing it. If she perceives that he really wants her to do something, she wants to do it. She thinks that that's love and he should feel the same way about her. But men have a gut-level resistance to doing what they're told, to doing what someone expects them to do. It's the opposite response of what women have.' She reminds readers that, of course, there are men who are very helpful toward their women. 'But if a man is going to be touchy, it's more likely to go in that direction. Whereas if a woman is insecure, she's more likely to go in the other direction, (and) be super-accommodating.'

Conflict: direct vs. avoidance

Men tend to handle conflict directly, again due to the competition and superiority programming. Women, however, often avoid and fear conflict. They have been taught not to hurt anybody's feelings. In many cases women will still engage in conflict, but only when they are threatened, and see no other alternative.

Looking at beliefs

Labels arise from our belief system. Our beliefs are largely stored in our subconscious and become a reality through our life experiences. The belief system is formed as a result of other people's beliefs combined with the circumstances of our past and leads to our life experiences, thus:

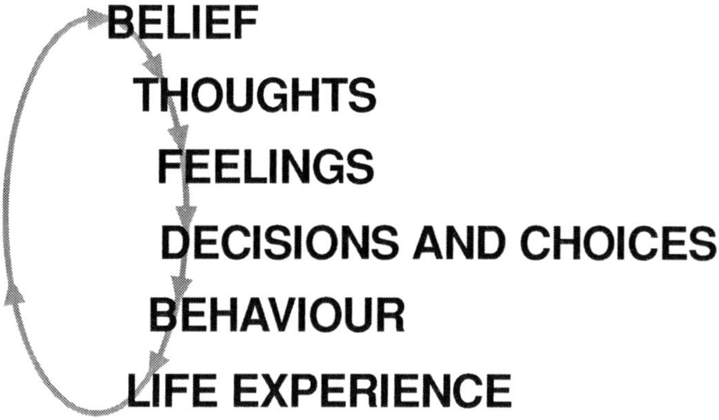

In order to survive, we had to adopt to the beliefs of our family and society's expectations. These beliefs include the rules and negative messages that we were taught and thus incorporated into our view of others and ourselves. Our beliefs may include:

- Men should be in charge
- Women are hysterical
- Men shouldn't show emotion
- It's not feminine to get angry
- Men always get aggressive
- A woman shouldn't run a business
- Men must have status
- Women shouldn't be ambitious
- Men must know everything
- A woman's place is in the home
- Women should earn less than their partners
- Men should earn high wages

Conditioning for gender expectations

The role of conditioning in our lives is crucial to the shaping of our identity. As children, we are dependent upon the adults in our life to feed, nurture and guide us. They pass onto us their beliefs, values and attitudes. As we grow, we absorb their teachings into our psyche and the subtle blending of external influences and our own internal character makes a heady rulebook for adult life.

We use role models through observation and mimicry of:

- values and beliefs about gender
- emotional and intellectual responses
- verbal communication styles
- gender-related behaviour
- gender-related dress.

During our formative years, our parents (or other primary people) provide the gender role models for us to begin moulding ourselves upon. There is always the struggle to rebel against our parents or to emulate them. However, we don't necessarily work through issues directly with our parents. Often we deal with them via other indirect sources such as lovers, friends or at work. If, for example, we grew up with a particularly controlling or critical parent, we may rebel against authority figures at work or be constantly seeking approval from them. As children, we want to be noticed and approved of by our parents and other role models. If we received constant disapproval and criticism when young, we are likely to constantly seek validation from others today. Not knowing how to approve of ourselves, by learning through example, can prevent us from discovering our own needs and wants. We look for reactions in others and assume what we must do is to please them. This may result in fearing failure and feeling unworthy, thus holding us back from fulfilment through work (or other life area).

Brief vs. detailed

Men, programmed to communicate only to keep people alive, to keep the species going, still generally speak briefly and to the point. Men communicate to solve problems, to figure things out (understand), whereas women communicate to bond, relate, and to be understood. So women discuss things in more detail.

Anima and animus

Now for some popular psychology to further explain the male and female.

The Anima This represents the female qualities within a man as learnt through the mother. The positive of the anima is that it keeps the man attuned to inner values and is a guide to his inner self and is intuitive, nurturing, creating and has feeling. The negative is that of irritability, depression, uncertainty, insecurity or touchiness. If the relationship with the mother was too strong, this may make the man weak willed or preyed upon by women. This image is responsible for man's image of women.

The Animus This represents the male qualities within a woman as learnt through the father. The negative is that of power, coldness, obstinacy and force. The positive is action, assertive, goal orientated and logical. This image is responsible for woman's image of men.

The anima and animus are the underdeveloped sides of the personality attempting to assert themselves for good or bad.

Within every woman's psyche dwells what is called the animus. The animus represents the male qualities within a female. Every man has the counterpart – an anima – the female qualities within a male. The female part (of men and women) intuitively creates the holding bay upon which the male part (of women and men) acts and produces form (see diagram overleaf).

For women, the larger part of their psyche is instinctive and receptive and it is the animus, the male side, which needs to be encouraged out in a positive way and blended with femaleness. The tendency is to have insight (female) and to act upon it aggressively (male) as we observe the male role models around us to do. The healthy way is to have insight and to act upon it assertively, referring back to the female for further insight and guidance to produce the right balance.

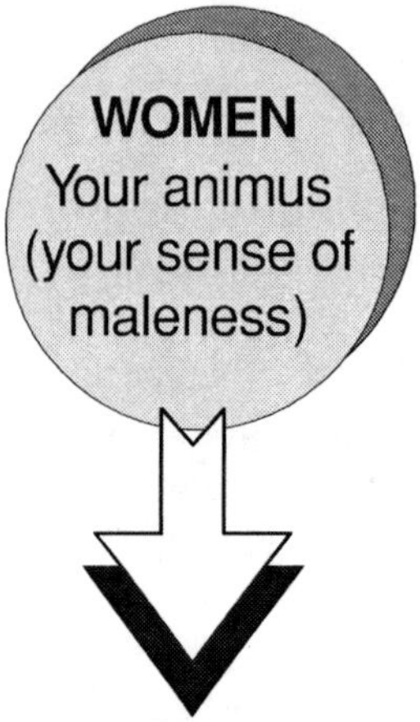

Females learn from the women in their childhood how to be female and how women use their sense of maleness. Females learn from the men in their childhood how to use maleness.

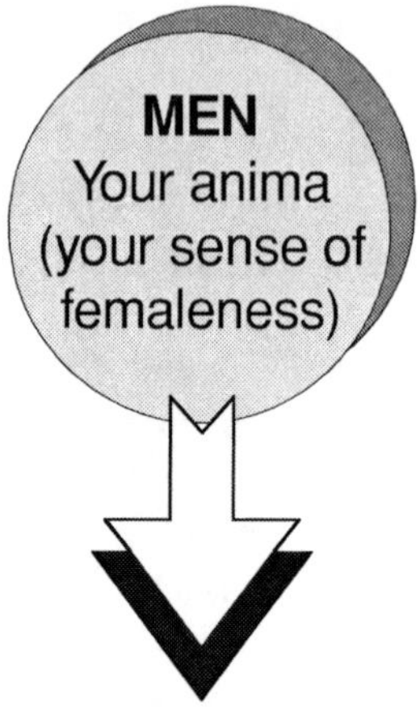

Males learn from the men in their childhood how to be male and how men use their sense of femaleness. Males learn from the women in their childhood how to use femaleness.

Men and women respond differently to new ideas

The book, *Women's Ways of Knowing*, by Belenky, Clinchy, Goldberger & Tarule (1986) describes a feminine learning style that fits well with women's conversational style. Example: when women hear a new or different idea, they set their doubts and disbelief aside and tune in carefully to what the person is saying; they try to see it from the other person's viewpoint. Women try to understand the other person's opinion as completely and deeply as possible; they cognitively 'go with them,' wanting to hear the person's views and to understand why they think this way. Women seek to make sense of the new idea, to grasp how it can be seen as accurate and useful. It involves empathising with the speaker to cooperatively assimilate the truth together, e.g. cooperating. Women effectively use this same listening style when someone has a personal problem.

Contrast this with a common male approach: When someone expresses a new idea or one males don't agree with, they start arguing in their head and to question the validity of everything 'How do you know that?' 'Is that logical?' 'Aren't there exceptions or other explanations or conclusions possible?' 'What are this person's motives and biases?' This is critical thinking; it is the essence of the scientific method; you could call it a doubting approach. Men like the intellectual game. It is like trying to find out who is superior. Women frequently dislike this kind of discourse, believing arguments don't influence anyone's thinking and reduce intimacy. Both are valuable skills.

Gender roles for men

The old male sex roles gave power and advantages to males but also created problems for men. Boys and men are much more free to express anger than any other emotion. This is related to their high rate (compared to females) of criticising, scapegoating, and attacking other people. Unfortunately, they are also three times more likely to be hyperactive than girls and they are more likely to believe their problems are caused by outside factors; whereas, females are more self-blaming. Males try to avoid problems; they distract themselves. In contrast, females talk out their problems with friends.

Besides the aggression-related problems of males, one can imagine many other problems: if you are expected to be superior, always perfectly in control of things, it is a constant strain to meet those standards. Also, if you are expected to be strong, unemotional, independent, competitive at work, it is hard to come home and be an interdependent equal, washing the dishes, bathing the kids, sharing your self-doubts and remorse about conflicts at work, and being soft and caringly intimate with others (Fasteau, 1974). Men are saying to women, 'if you like the drive, intellect, and toughness that gets me promoted and a Mercedes, why do you expect me to be completely different as a dinner partner? You can't have both!' The truth is maybe you can have both, but the point is: some men feel as dehumanised when they are judged by their job or income or car as women feel when they are judged by their weight, or breasts or clothes.

If a male alone is expected to provide well for a family, he will ordinarily have little time to relax and enjoy home life, little time to get to know his own children. Men need freedom from all the financial responsibility for the family, freedom from the demand that they be a 'real men and not cry or be sissies,' freedom from the urge to compete and prove their superiority in every interaction, freedom to be equally involved with child care, freedom to have intimate friendships, freedom from being held responsible for the female's sexual satisfaction, freedom from having their personal worth being based almost entirely on their success at work, etc. (Farrell, 1975, 1993).

Males who adopt extremely macho traits and superior attitudes run the risk of several other major problems (Stillson, O'Neil & Owen, 1991). For example, the highly masculine stereotype has been shown to be associated with family violence, delinquency, fights while drinking, child sexual abuse, and rape. The macho male suppresses feelings and, thus, has more health and psychological problems as well as more superficial and fragile relationships. These facts should help the tough, loud, dominating, belligerent male re-consider his life style. It is certainly to the credit of enlightened males that they have moved away from the destructive aspects of the highly masculine sex role stereotypes, but Robert Bly (1990) believes many men have become 'soft' in the process and lost their resolve to do what they think is right. Guard against confusing being good (sensitive to others' needs, assertive, strong, and cooperative) with being weak (self-depreciating, scared, and self-absorbed).

Perhaps the major spokesperson during the 1980s on male issues has been Herb Goldberg (1976, 1980), a psychologist who denounces the traditional tough, silent, unfeeling, unempathic man. He thinks men are killing themselves by trying to be 'true' men. Instead, men should get in touch with their feelings, their bodies, their close relationships (or lack of them), and their basic purposes in life. Goldberg thinks men should stay assertive and independent, but increase their sensitivity to others, their inner awareness of emotions and values, and their commitment to others. In short, they wouldn't become less of a 'man' but rather a more complete, wiser, caring man (Fanning & McKay, 1994).

More male-female differences

- Colour-blindness, haemophilia, leukaemia, dyslexia and left-handedness are more common in males.
- Sex differences start early, e.g. infant girls seem to see faces better and are more responsive to people than boys are. Even as adults, research has shown that women can read non-verbal cues and most emotions better than men (not anger).
- Certain diseases plague women such as thyroid and bladder disorders, anaemia's, spastic colon, varicose veins, migraines, gallstones, arthritis, asthma.
- Men have deadlier problems such as heart disease, strokes, emphysema and more visual-hearing defects.
- Women live 7 years longer, although are sick more often.
- When men and women have strokes on the left side, where language functions are thought to be, men are three times more likely to become aphasic (speech problems). This suggests speech is more concentrated on the left side in males than in females. Male and female brains may differ but the innate intellectual differences seem to be very slight.

Valuing Diversity

Stereotypes involve generalisations about the 'typical' characteristics of members of a group, e,g,

Jane is a female, so she probably has characteristics x, y and z.

Prejudice arises from an attitude toward the members of some group based solely on their membership in that group.

Once stereotyping behaviour is activated, this will affect the information we attend to and, therefore, notice and process. Stereotypes obviously affect social judgments we make about others.

- They influence how much we like the person.
- They colour our expectations regarding probability of certain behaviours in the person.
- They are reflected in the mood the person 'puts' us in.

Prejudice in the workplace could come from men or women. Traditionally, men regard the workplace as a male-dominated area and, as more women enter the world of commerce and industry, resentment and confusion is going to increase.

Every one of us, to a certain extent, believes some of the old gender stereotypes. Especially if stereotypes are viewed as descriptions of general behaviour tendencies. Regardless of the significant progress in diversity issues being made throughout the workforce, stereotypes of some sort will always exist. The important thing to remember is that the simple presence of stereotypes is not the problem. The problem occurs when stereotypes are used, however subconsciously, to prejudge people's abilities and competence and to develop unfair and incorrect expectations. When that happens, effective communication, along with productive relationships, is jeopardised and thwarted.

Our bias and prejudice are deeply rooted within us. From the moment we are born, we learn about our environment, the world, and ourselves. Families, friends, peers, books, teachers, idols, and others influence us on what is right and what is wrong. These early learnings are deeply rooted within us and shape our perceptions about how we view things and how we respond to them. What we learn and experience gives us our subjective point of view known as bias. Our biases serve as filtering devices that allow us to make sense of new information and experiences based on what we already know. Many of our biases are good as they allow us to assume that something is true without proof. Otherwise, we would have to start learning anew on everything that we do. But, if we allow our bias to shade our perceptions of what people are capable of, then the bias is harmful. We start prejudging others on what we think that they cannot do.

The following exercise will help demonstrate the effect of seemingly innocent stereotypes on judgements of others. Very quickly, using your first impression, indicate beside each adjective below which sex the word best describes. Use M for male, F for female, and B for both only if the word immediately brings to mind both men and women.

horseback rider	skydiver
impetuous	impatient
too sensitive	persistent
assertive	intense
nurturing	committed
talkative	hates spiders
dynamic	aggressive
outspoken	compassionate
driven	logical
intuitive	gentle
warm	likes flowers
self-starter	emotional
competitive	football fan
entrepreneur	scuba diver
critical	hiker
funny	cheerful

likes children	lifeguard
intelligent	good cook
romantic	fussy
fashionable	independent
daring	competent

Looking over your responses, notice the number of Ms, Fs and Bs. Most people get a good mix of all three. Looking at the list of adjectives, is there any one word that could not describe either sex? If not, then all the Ms and Fs recorded indicate subconscious (and sometimes not so subconscious) stereotypical beliefs. Keep in mind that simply believing that some of these descriptions are gender-based is not wrong. Stereotypes, after all, develop from observed behavioural generalities. For example, probably close to 100% of those completing this exercise are likely to indicate F for the descriptions of emotional and nurturing and M for the words aggressive and competitive. Speaking in general terms, are women usually more emotional than men, at least from what others can see? Maybe so. Are men usually more outwardly competitive than women? Yes. Again, the stereotypes of themselves are not the problem. However, if stereotypes are used to form opinions about other elements of a person's capabilities or behaviour, then problems arise. Doing so is judgmental and assumptive. Reviewing the list again, could it be describing one person? Could that person be a man or a woman? Most people agree that, yes, the list could be describing a man or a woman.

The key point demonstrated by this exercise is this: just because a woman may be emotional, too sensitive in certain situations, nurturing, and a good cook, does not preclude her from also being decisive, competent, intelligent, and driven. And just because a man might be decisive, aggressive, logical, and independent does not mean that he is not also nurturing, sensitive, gentle in certain situations, and a good cook.

Working with diversity

Diversity is one of the most vital aspects of the Learning Company. How a company manages to work with the diversity it has is one of the keys to learning and productivity. For many years companies have tried to suppress diversity, preferring sameness and uniformity because this is easier to manage. ... How can we positively use the differences between us to create power in the Learning Company?

M. Pedler et al.

A TRAINING EXERCISE – TO RECOGNISE THE VALUE OF DIVERSITY IN AN ORGANISATION

1 Find out the criteria for diversity

Gather together a group of about 12-20 men and women. Facilitate a discussion on recognising the value of diversity in an organisation. Discuss the different types of diversity, e.g. gender.

2 Acknowledge the importance of differences

Divide the group into smaller, mixed groups to answer the following four sentences:

- What's important to me about being a woman is –
  What's important to me about being a man is –
- As a woman, I bring to this organisation –
  As a man, I bring to this organisation –
- Our organisation empowers me to live out my special character as a woman by –
  Our organisation empowers me to live out my special character as a man by –
- What I like about the others in our organisation (who are different in the respective sense), is –

3 Summarise

Return to the larger group and summarise the results.

Diversity is about empowering people. It makes an organisation effective by capitalising on all the strengths of each employee. Diversity is understanding, valuing, and using the differences in every person. Embracing diversity is the first item for building teams. Every team building theory states that to build a great team, there must be a diverse group of people on the team, that is, you must avoid choosing people who are only like you. Choosing people like yourself to be on teams is similar to inbreeding – it multiplies the flaws – while the other end of the continuum is having an assorted group of individuals, which diminishes the flaws of others.

Embracing diversity is more than tolerating people who are different. It means actively welcoming and involving them, by:

- **encouraging people to ask for support.** Because we each have different backgrounds (personal and professional), when we are in a group with others, we may feel alienated by our experiences and reluctant to ask for clarification with issues or support with problems that don't appear to fit in with the 'norm'.
- **actively seeking information** from people from a variety of backgrounds and cultures. Also, including everyone on the problem solving and decision making process.
- **creating a team spirit** which every member feels a part of.

Diversity is not only black and white, female and male, homosexual and heterosexual, Jew and Christian, young and old and so on, but the diversity of every individual, slow learner and fast learner, introvert and extrovert, scholar and sports-person, liberal and conservative ...

A realistic ideal of cultural diversity is one of multiculturalism. **Multiculturalism** is based on the idea that cultural identities should not be discarded, but instead, should be maintained and valued. The importance of cultural diversity has been, in large, accepted in business. This is illustrated by the increased presence of women and minorities in the business world.

Cultural diversity matters to every single one of us, both professionally and personally. For our businesses and communities to not only survive, but to thrive, each of us needs to be aware of and sensitive to all the members of the community. When all segments are respected and utilised, it benefits everyone involved. A great many of us live on the margins of society. To be in a margin means that you are not a part of the mainstream, popular culture. In this nation, our popular culture, or ideal for business success, is white, young, heterosexual, Christian and male. This means you are on the margins if you are:

- a woman
- have any ethnic background that is non-white
- are not a heterosexual
- are not a Christian
- are not between the ages of 21-40

If you can answer yes to any one of these criteria, you live in the margins. This means that there are obstacles, prejudices, and stereotypes about you as an individual. You cannot automatically assume that society's view of you is unobstructed or based solely on your individual character, qualifications or accomplishments.

The management of diversity can be considered a response to the need to recognise, respect and capitalise on the different backgrounds in our society in terms of race, ethnicity, and gender. Different cultural groups have different values, styles, and personalities, each of which may have a substantial effect on the way they do business. Valuing diversity happens from the inside out. When we can embrace our inner diversities, e.g. we like to eat meat but can't bear the thought of blood sports, we are better placed to accept the diversities of those around us. When we can each accept ourselves and the diversities within others, we are going to find it easier to work together with our differences.

Work-place prejudice based on gender

Broadly speaking, women tend to be concentrated in lower status, lower income jobs, and earn less than men in the same occupations. Why? Expectations, self-confidence and negative reactions to female leaders (there still is an invisible glass ceiling). Women tend to express lower self-confidence than men in many achievement-related situations. This may lead to supervisors viewing women employees as less determined to succeed on the job than men, and may contribute to women not receiving promotions to full equality in the workplace.

Negative reactions to female leaders

While most people agree that women can be effective leaders, people do not hold female leaders in as high regard or evaluate them as favourably as male leaders. Negative evaluations are particularly likely:

- when women adapt a masculine leadership style
- when the evaluators are males
- when most leaders in the field are men.

Transforming negative attitudes

You have no control over another person's attitude or beliefs. But you have control over your own. By your own thoughts, feelings and behaviours, you give an impression to your colleagues, superiors and subordinates of who you are. If you work with bigoted people who try to belittle you, put you down, harass you or try take away your power, it is up to you to keep faith with yourself. It goes something like this:

Thought	John/Mary is trying to undermine my authority by telling me I can't do my work when I know I can
Feeling	frustration, anger
Decision/choice	to go to my boss and get his or her support or to assertively tell John/Mary that my work is my responsibility
Life experience	self respect *plus* a sense that my work is under my control *plus* a work colleague knows he or she can't ride rough-shod over me *plus* confidence in the support of my boss

When people see you behaving assertively and with confidence, they have two choices. They can either respect you, however grudgingly or they can carry on in their bigoted way. Just because you play by a set of fair rules, doesn't necessarily mean other people will. Hopefully they will but if they don't, you then have two choices. To accept the way they are and to carry on being assertive, knowing that life won't always be easy with them or to get away from them. You've got the power. You decide.

Working with patriarchs

A patriarchal society is a male dominated culture. Attitudes may include:

- male values rule, e.g. wealth, competition and aggression
- men are leaders while women follow
- it's okay for a woman to gain power by default, e.g. Indira Ghandi
- the male has a greater value than the female.

Women's support

To a greater extent, women have supported a patriarchal society. Women have believed that they need to be protected, that they have a limited value and that it is wrong to have a position of power by merit alone. Women tend to collude by putting others first, maintaining harmony, by doing much of society's unpaid work and by being the backbone of family and working man. Some tips on how to cope with patriarchs include:

- limit contact time
- get on with the job
- when you have contact time, deal in facts, calmly and assertively
- stay in control
- you don't have to prove anything
- get support from other superiors
- he's not your father – don't feel like a child
- you are a skilled woman in your own right.

Working with women

Women can be bitchy and underhand. With a man in business, you usually know where you stand, although there are exceptions to the rule. Most women in positions of authority are up front but again, there are the exceptions. Suggestions when working with women include:

- be direct
- be firm
- allow for the talking through of issues to resolution
- be an active listener
- acknowledge her contributions and act upon them if appropriate.

15 QUESTIONS TO ASK ABOUT A POSITIVE DIVERSITY STRATEGY

1 Do you have a workplace inclusivity strategic plan?

2 Do you have formal policies and procedures in place for promoting your inclusive work environment?

3 Have you made the business case for all of your diversity initiatives?

4 Have you done your research on internal and external customer data?

5 Do you have a workplace inclusivity/diversity advisory or steering committee (ad-hoc employee group)?

6 Are you studying best practices, e.g. what are other organisations doing within the industry and outside of the industry?

7 Do you have family-friendly policies put in place, e.g. flexitime, telecommuting, job sharing, paternity leave, etc.?

8 Do you conduct structured group interviews for open management positions?

9 Have you developed an in-house diversity resource centre complete with books, videos, newsletter, and other educational materials like multicultural calendars and made all of this available to your employees?

10 Do you have a formal, fully inclusive mentoring programme?

11 Are you attempting to diversify your recruiting pool while maintaining high standards?

12 Are you acknowledging and celebrating the diversity within your employment ranks before attempting to value and manage your diversity (events, activities, etc.)?

13 Do you offer more advanced courses in gender communications, problem-solving, and conflict management for diverse employees?

14 Have you completed sexual harassment prevention training for all of your employees?

15 Are you conducting diversity training for managers, supervisors, and employees?

The Role of Gender in Business

The managing director of a company might complain that his senior women have a tendency to come into his office, dump all their problems and leave. Frustrated he says - 'I pay them to solve problems, not give them back to me'. This is a typical example of the different way men and women operate. The woman is discussing the issues with him. She knows she needs to find the answers but talking about it helps her work out the solutions. Meanwhile he has moved straight into solution mode. 'Once I'm told about a problem I have to solve it'. The result is that he's feeling frustrated because he now thinks he's got to do her job. She's feeling frustrated because she thinks he is taking away her responsibility.

Differences in communication styles

So what are the differences in communication styles? Generally speaking, men use language to preserve their independence and maintain their position in the group; women use language to create connection and intimacy. Next time you are in a mixed business meeting, notice the dynamics. Basically there seems to be two styles:

- The **Information Style** is often associated with men. Talk is primarily a means to preserve independence and negotiate and maintain status.
- The **Relationship Style** is often associated with women. Conversation is primarily a language of rapport: a way of establishing connections and negotiating relationships.

Communication is a key issue facing today's organisations. Differences in gender communication styles can affect what gets done, how it gets done, who gets heard, who gets acknowledged, and who gets credit. Consider that:

- Men and women have radically different ideas of what it means to be a team player.
- Meeting behaviours are different. For men, the meeting often doesn't happen *in* the meeting and women may not know this.
- Not understanding these differences creates systemic barriers – barriers that negatively impact individual productivity, morale, and job satisfaction. Not to mention that inhibiting employee contribution has a negative impact on your organisation's bottom line.
- Women often use disclaimers, hedges, and tag questions in their linguistic behaviour, which can backfire when talking to men.
- Men and women communicate, approach work place challenges, solve problems, and provide leadership in remarkably different ways. What is interpreted as assertive in a man can be viewed as aggressive in a woman.
- Non-verbal communication is different. For example, when women nod it means 'I hear you,' while men nod in agreement.

Misunderstandings and miscommunications between men and women happen every day, for two reasons. First, we have different communication styles. Second, we think that everyone communicates in the same way. Awareness, understanding, and valuing our different communication styles removes barriers created by misunderstandings. It ensures that men and women are flexible and able to adapt to different situations. It impacts on their ability to work together, as well as their ability to get ahead in the organisation. In other words, it affects their productivity. Understanding and valuing our different communication styles will result in:

- successful communications
- the reduction of gender conflicts
- the improvement of working relationships
- increased productivity.

Body language

Even in body language, men and women can give off different signals. A female colleague, who is an executive at a large PR firm in the City, expressed it well. She recalled a meeting of senior executives that morning, half men and half women. 'To my horror, I noticed that all the women were nodding and saying things like *yes*, *okay*, *I understand*, while the men just sat straight-faced and wrote the occasional note,' she said. 'The men were totally focused on the task at hand. The women were working hard to relate to the speaker rather than focusing on what he was actually saying'. Women nodding during a conversation usually means 'I understand what you are saying'. Men nodding in a discussion usually means 'I agree with you'. Often problems arise when a man misinterprets a woman's automatic rapport-building nodding, as meaning that she's in agreement – when in fact she may not be.

> The only way we can get other people to change, since we cannot control their behaviour, is to change our own behaviour. In order to do this, we need to 'speak' gender differences.
>
> Dr. Pat Heim

Decision making

Think about the different styles of approach when a male and female manager is asked to make a decision. The woman will tend to discuss it with others, seek their input and feedback before making a recommendation to senior management. She thinks it is important that everyone feels they have contributed to the decision and therefore are more likely to support it. In contrast the man usually makes the decision, with discreet consultation, and makes the recommendation. He believes that actively seeking input takes away from his position. He's in charge so he needs to make the decision. Because of this, it is likely that he will think that she cannot make a decision on her own, and needs to check with others first. Very different approaches for very different reasons. The female's first priority is relationship. The male's is status.

Gender perceptions

In a working environment, the way that co-workers perceive each other is essential to create a positive atmosphere. Every person does not perceive or interpret information in the same way, especially between males and females. Two basic perceptual processes are useful to managers:

1 **Selective perception.** This is a process of screening out information that people are not comfortable with or is contradicting to one's values. Positive perceptions of fellow co-workers are a necessity in the work environment. A person's life, gender, and work experiences form their selective perception.

2 **Stereotyping.** This is the labelling of a person we perceive to have certain personal characteristics. Stereotyping can be positive or negative. The word *perceive* is defined as the process to become aware of through the senses or the understanding. Everyone in the world is different and this means that nobody will perceive occurrences or people in the same manner. People in the work environment, and people in general, view men and women differently.

Attitudes

Men and women are often perceived with different attitudes when they cross the stereotypical boundary lines. For example, a man is considered ambitious while a woman who uses the same style and method might be perceived as pushy. To turn the situation around, when looking at a man and woman who are concerned with their employees, well-being, a woman might be perceived as sensitive while her male counterpart might be perceived as wimpy.

☯ When a staff member expresses frustration by crying in the office, do observers quietly doubt her competence on the job?

☯ When a TQM consultant interrupts his client several times during a phone call to discuss an upcoming project, is he automatically assumed to be quite rude and insensitive?

☯ If a new training manager brought homemade cake to the office, would others question her management and decision-making skills?

☯ If an outspoken, driven, aggressive sales director mentioned he had two children, would some people wonder, at some level, if he were a good and loving father?

An employee may express emotion differently than her manager does, and that's fine. Her emotion does not necessarily translate to poor management abilities. The sales director certainly seems like a focused, driven, aggressive man. But chances are that he turns those hard-charging sales qualities off when he goes home to be with his children.

TIP BOX ♀⇨♂

WOMEN COMMUNICATING WITH MEN

The statements below are adapted from *The Androgynous Manager*, by Alice G. Sargent, Amacom, 1981:

- Stop self-limiting behaviours, such as allowing interruptions or laughing after making a serious statement.
- Practice taking risks and overcoming fear.
- Learn to state exactly what you want and face the risk of being cut down or wrong, especially at meetings. This is not a 'safe' position, but it is an honest one. Be concerned more about stating your own position than about how the other person is reacting to you.
- Stop feeling comfortable with being a victim and suffering.
- State your own needs and do not back down even if the immediate response is not acceptance.
- Learn to focus on a task and regard it as at least as important as the relationship among the people doing the task.
- Stop turning anger and blame inward. Stop making negative statements about yourself. Make positive statements.

The sexes are saturated with, even defined by, many differences. Stereotypical, evolutionary, biological and social differences, to name a few. It's no wonder a 'gender gap' exists, especially when it comes to communication. Closing the gap is possible, however, and certainly desirable as more women enter the workforce and move higher within the ranks of their companies. The benefits of improved communication between men and women at work are numerous. These positive outcomes can include more effective teamwork, better sales results, more satisfied customers, higher job satisfaction, increased harmony and lower stress, and even reduced sexual harassment problems – all consistent with human resource goals.

Building positive work relationships

Pointers in developing positive work relationships with someone of the opposite gender (or anyone come to that) include:

- Don't expect closeness through inappropriate behaviour. Pouting, withdrawing, being curt, negative and whiney seldom draw people closer. Own up to your emotions and feelings and express them in an open, honest, clear and direct way.
- Learn to praise and accept praise. Say nice things about a person's character, not just about how nice they look. If you don't accept praise, people will stop giving it after a while.
- When confronted, listen to what the person has to say without the typical defensive, reactive self in each of us. No one likes to be criticised, but change does not occur until one is self-aware, and self-awareness involves feedback. Learn to ask for feedback.
- Learn to be direct, open, and clear in giving messages. Don't be afraid to express your negative emotions. The key to self-expression is how you state your feelings. Most relationships are strengthened through creative use of conflict.
- Make time for others. Time is a matter of priorities. If you want to do something badly enough for yourself or another, you will make the time.
- Learn to set limits with yourself and others. Avoid being the rescuer or doormat. Not setting limits leads to resentment.

- Be tolerant of the weaknesses in others.
- Be tolerant of your own weaknesses. Don't be self-critical in front of another, because after awhile both of you will believe it.
- Be a good listener.
- You don't have to justify your every move in life. An honest response is appropriate, but avoid feeling the need to make excuses for your actions,
- Don't cop-out if you have a responsibility when someone is depending on you. If the world gets angry with you, it may be because you have become undependable.
- Whenever you suppress a feeling, it will eventually manifest itself magnified many times over. Beware of depression, illness or emotional outbursts as expressions of suppression.
- Remember that 30% of your communication is non-verbal. Be in touch with the messages your body language, voice inflection, posture, and facial expressions give.
- Avoid 'winning' situations. If you win a discussion, it's at the expense of someone, and now you have to deal with that person's feelings. No one is right all the time.
- Come to accept the fact that not all of life's conflicts, including your own, may be resolvable, whether in the present or future. Some people and things simply can't or don't want to change. Don't expect yourself or another to alter behaviour without proper know-how and motivation.

TIP BOX ♀⇨♂

TIP BOX

WOMEN COMMUNICATING WITH MEN

- Speak up! Don't allow men to interrupt you. Stand up for yourself.
- Avoid using tag endings that make you sound unsure of yourself such as 'don't you think?' and 'is that okay?'
- Don't take male comments so personally. They don't, and can't understand why you do! Remember that most men are direct in their communication and like to get straight to the point.
- Focus on being logical in the way you present your information and avoid giving unnecessary details (storytelling).
- Avoid discussing anything too personal. Instead talk about job-related issues and current affairs.
- Tell it how it is. Don't dilute your comments or criticism. Men get confused if you try to soften your feedback by focusing first on what they did right or what you liked. Be direct.
- Don't try to be one of the boys - they don't like it.
- Stop saying 'I'm sorry' just to be polite. Only apologise if you are wrong.
- Monitor your body language and facial expressions. Be aware of giggling or smiling when it's not appropriate.
- Lighten-up. Don't take things too seriously or hold grudges. Learn to separate business matters from your personal feelings.

TIP BOX ♂⇨♀

MEN COMMUNICATING WITH WOMEN

- Invest time in building rapport.
- Focus on being more polite by using words such as 'please' and 'thank you' when making a request or giving an order.
- Avoid monopolising conversations, speaking for the woman or interrupting her.
- Be aware that because relationships are important to women they tend to take things more personally. What you consider is just direct communication can seem harsh to them.
- Avoid barking out commands or orders to women. They prefer, and respond better, to polite requests.
- Don't call a woman names like 'honey', 'dear' or 'darling'. Unless they know you very well, they will probably think you are chauvinistic and condescending.
- Control any outbursts of anger or frustration. Women are uncomfortable when men yell and curse.
- Pay attention when women are speaking. Use good eye contact, nod and use 'I'm listening' type of sounds like 'uhuh'.
- Encourage women to speak more succinctly by asking questions or bringing them back to the point.
- Be aware of the subconscious influence of your mother! If you have a negative reaction to a woman at work notice if you are responding to things about her that remind you of your mother.

Management, Leadership and Gender

Management

Good management requires that we all must be aware of managing diversity in the workplace. Researchers and professionals working in the field of gender issues have documented differences in men's and women's approaches or perspectives at work and much advancement has taken place within the work environment during the last thirty years. An essential component to help promote a healthy working environment is to be aware of different perceptions and how these affect the working environment. A manager must also be unbiased to personal opinion and be able to provide an atmosphere that does not include any form of stereotyping. Here are a couple of thought provokers:

- A study by Donnell and Hall in 1980 indicated that women managers reported lower basic needs and higher needs for self-actualisation. When they compared that data with the male data, the female managers were more occupied with opportunities for growth, autonomy, and challenge and less concerned with work environment and pay. Donnell and Hall concluded that women managers exhibited a more mature and higher-achieving motivational profile than males (Ivencevich, Matteson).

- Supervisors may use an informal technique of evaluation that enhances the gender differences between men and women in the workplace (Williams). The way that a manager or supervisor perceives a person to be has a major influence on people. A quality that a man possesses may be viewed with high praise, while a woman may be denigrated, or vice-versa.

Manager traits

A manager:

- innovates by tinkering with existing processes
- has an instinct for survival; seeks to minimise risks and tolerate the mundane
- doesn't insure imagination, creativity, or ethical behaviour
- uses an accumulation of collective experience to get where he or she is going
- sees the world as relatively impersonal and static
- rationally analyses a situation, developing systematic selection of goals and purposes
- finds harmony in living up to society's, company and family's expectations
- has a low level of emotional involvement in the work
- directs energy toward goals, resources, and organisation structure, determining the problems to be solved
- views work as something that must be done or tolerated
- views work as an enabling process, involving a combination of ideas, skills, timing and people
- influences people through the use of logic, facts and reason.
- sees him or herself as conservator and regulator of an existing order of affairs; belongs to the organisation; believes in duty and responsibility to the organisation.
- becomes anxious when there is relative disorder
- focuses on how things need to be done
- relates to people by the role they play in a sequence or in a decision making process
- focuses attention on procedure
- develops him or herself through socialisation, seeking to maintain the balance of social relations
- sees him or herself as an integral part of the social structure and social standard

Leadership

The autonomy and distancing effect of a 'lone leader' approach may partly explain our ambivalent reactions to leadership and leaders. While we have certain expectations of leadership, we become resistant if we feel that leadership takes away our control. At the same time, we often demand leadership or we have a desire for someone else to assume responsibility. If we continue to focus power 'at the top', we create a dynamic that reinforces the emergence of people who then need to control and may enjoy exercising that power.

Leaders and leadership do not exist in vacuums. If we consider leadership to be less an attribute of an individual and more the influence that emerges through reciprocal actions, we may be able to find ways for more people to be a part of leadership. When shared leadership occurs, people approach problems in collaborative ways, engaging each other in defining the work to be done, facilitating interaction and sustaining action so that goals can be realised. People come to focus on the work itself rather than on who has authority to do it. Shared leadership directs; it does not dictate.

People in designated leadership positions need to find different ways of being accountable without acting to control others. These individuals need to understand their own strengths and weaknesses in order to feel comfortable learning from others, rather than always needing to know the answers. Ideally, these leaders draw on the leadership skills throughout the system while creating conditions that allow others to see their own roles in leadership. Such conditions mean moving from where only a few people have authority to more open structures where information, relationships and connections are fluid. We bring energy and commitment to our work if we feel valued and included with a shared sense of ownership. And we are more able to support activities that we help to create. This interactive process of leadership holds more promise for the transformation of our work in changing organisations than do the top-down patterns of traditional leadership.

If we can move from an idea of leadership in someone else to seeing our own roles in being accountable for the work, we begin to change the dynamics of traditional leadership. We each also need to understand how we become accountable to the group for our actions. Can we help each other to operate fully as part of the larger whole? Can we work with others so they can exert influence over problems and solutions?

Leader traits

A leader:

- uses personal power to influence the thoughts and actions of others
- innovates through flashes of insight or intuition
- influences people through altering moods, evoking images and expectation
- directs energy toward guiding people toward practical solutions
- sees the world as full of colour, and constantly blending into new colours and shapes
- often jumps to conclusions, without a logical progression of thoughts or facts
- relates to people in intuitive and empathic ways
- views work as developing fresh approaches to old problems, or finding new options for old issues
- sometimes reacts to the mundane and routine as an affliction
- focuses on what needs to be done, leaving decisions to people involved
- shows intuitive, mystical understanding of what needs to be done
- views work as something challenging and exciting
- works to develop harmonious interpersonal relationships
- focuses on the decision to be made
- works best when things are somewhat disorderly or chaotic
- forms intensive one-on-one relationships, which may be of short duration; often has mentors
- takes in emotional signals from others, making them mean something in the relationship with an individual
- is often passionate about the work
- finds self-esteem through self-reliance and personal expression
- communicates through 'messages' heightening the emotional response

- sees him or herself as separate from the environment; may work in organisations but never belong to them; searches for opportunities for change.
- is able to tolerate aggressive interchanges, encouraging emotional involvement with others
- develops self through personal mastery, struggling for psychological and social change
- sees him or herself as a constantly evolving human being, focusing more inwardly than outwardly.

Leadership can be a lonely role and a key to being an effective leader is in coming to terms with the responsibility it entails. As you are the pivot for providing vision and support to others, you need a network of support yourself such as mentors, colleagues, family and friends. It is also important to understand that you may be a leader in a particular sphere but this doesn't necessarily make you a suitable leader in all spheres.

Effective leaders:

- have a strong belief in their own and other people's capabilities and set out to release this latent power in others and themselves
- respect others and believe that they, given the opportunity, will contribute to the success of the organisation through their own inner conviction and drive
- personalise rather than generalise their leadership approach, in that they do not seek or use a single best practice approach but set out to create an empathetic relationship in which leader behaviour matches the needs of those being led
- democratise hierarchical work environments by using the structures, processes and procedures to strengthen and enable people rather than control them
- enthuse their followers and put enthusiasm into everything they do
- act as protectors of others in supporting their people from attack from outside interests
- through a process of tutoring and mentoring, develop the self esteem of people so they have the potential to become effective achievers themselves

- release the latent self-leadership capability of their people, so that they behave in ways that encourage them to take charge of their environment and take responsibility for their own actions
- manage by using an effective combination of direction, delegation and listening
- enhance the worth of their people by ensuring they are in tune with the environment and are producing effective outcomes

Effective leadership is a balancing act. The pivot is the task that needs to be completed while the balancing act is in the facilitation of personnel needed for completion. A leader may need to balance one individual, several apparently unconnected individuals or a specific team of individuals while focusing throughout on the task.

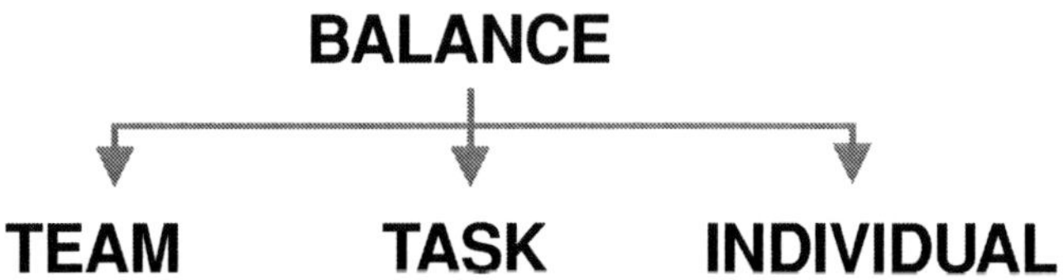

Robert Tannenbaum and Warren Schmidt have identified the following six leadership styles:

Tell	leader tells the team what to do and they have no say
Sell	leader tells the team what to do and gives reasons for the action and they have no say
Test	leader puts forward their solution or decision and asks for the agreement of the team
Consult	leader explain the situation, suggests a solution and asks the team for their solutions
Join	leader explain the situation and then joins the team to explore and discuss possible solutions
Delegate	leader explains the situation and asks the team to come up with possible solutions but takes no part in the discussion, agreeing only to accept the team's conclusions

Meredith Belbin has produced some excellent research on team leadership (and team roles). A concept of leadership styles is provided here:

The Motivator
Enthusiastic
Sympathetic
Influential
Charismatic
Social
Dramatic
Friendly
Generous
Fatal Flaw: Talks too much

The Supporter
Likeable
Team player
Predictable
Deliberate
Loyal
Patient
Low risk taker
Easy going
Fatal Flaw: Agrees too much

The Perfectionist
Conscientious
Orderly
Self-disciplined
Mature
High standards
Fretful
Accurate
Systematic
Fatal flaw: Questions too much

The Director
Ambitious
Risk-taker
Forceful
Powerful
Responsible
Energising
Organiser
Self-confidant
Fatal flaw: Directs too much

Leadership and gender stereotypes

Numerous perspectives have been used in research on leadership. Some psychologists have taken a trait-based approach to leadership. This approach states that leaders have certain personality attributes that their followers do not. For instance, leaders may be described as assertive, confident, tactful, or persuasive. Another approach addresses the behaviours of leaders such as initiating structure and consideration. Another approach sees leadership as situation-specific. Situational leadership theory states that the balance of initiating structure vs. consideration behaviours in which a leader must engage depends on the emotional maturity and expertise of the followers.

The general model of leadership perceptions proposes that leader behaviour is interpreted and labelled by followers; if the behaviour matches the followers' leadership prototype, the label of leader is applied to this person. For instance, an employee may view a leader as someone who takes charge of a situation and defines for the group how work should be done. Someone from the group who takes charge and structures the task at hand is likely to be perceived by this employee as a leader. Subsequent behaviour by this emergent leader is likely to reinforce perceptions of leadership. Being seen as a leader is important; followers who perceive another as a leader grant influence. This influence should enhance attainment of outcomes. Attainment of outcomes, in a reciprocal fashion, also affects follower perceptions. Being associated with positive (or negative) outcomes affects how strongly a person is seen as a leader.

General behaviour from men and women is perceived differently. Perceivers attach labels to the same behaviours enacted by men and women. One reason is because of gender stereotype. The leadership perceptions approach also helps to explain why it is sometimes difficult for people to accept women as leaders in the workplace. The traits often attached to effective leadership are 'masculine' qualities such as courage, persuasiveness, and assertiveness.

> Women's leadership styles tend to be web-like as opposed to the more male style of a family tree type of leadership. Women are more inclined to balance and share power through empowering others. Men tend to have a hierarchy.

Gender-based stereotypes include beliefs about expected interpersonal behaviour, and the types of roles or jobs best suited for men and women. The basic message in this is that followers interpret the same behaviour enacted by men and women differently. Follower perceptions depend on or are contingent on the leader's gender. For example, an assertive and competitive man is likely to be seen as leader-like, whereas the same behaviour on the part of a woman is likely to result in the label of 'bitch.' This is because gender stereotypes provide certain expectations of male and female behaviour. When those expectations are violated (as in the case of a women acting assertively), it results in dislike and a negative label being applied to describe her.

Currently, there are several major theories of leadership that are recognised and accepted. Here is a thumbnail sketch of leadership, past to present:

Trait theory

The first theory of leadership is trait theory, which arose around the turn of the century and held strong until the 1950s (Schriesheim & Neider, 1989). The goal of this theory was to identify a set of characteristics that distinguished leaders from non-leaders. The characteristics identified were considered to be specific to a person's personality; therefore suggesting that people were born leaders. Scholars identifying with trait theory were able to find certain common traits that leaders possess, e.g. intelligence, but were unable to create a set list that would screen people as effective or non-effective leaders.

Behavioural theory

The next major theory to rise was the behavioural theory. Behavioural theory was similar to trait theory in that theorists wanted to identify a 'set' pertaining to leadership, but the 'set' wanting to be identified described leadership *styles*, not traits. Theorists identified the diverse styles of leadership, and then sought a specific style, which would be effective in all situations. Just as with trait theory, scholars found several effective styles, but were unable to find a specific style that was best in all situations.

Contingency/leader substitutes

Contingency and leader substitutes theories have some common characteristics. Both work on the premise of the relationship between the leader, the situation, and the followers. The major difference between the two lies in the fact that contingency uses the three factors as determinants of effective leadership, whereas leader substitutes uses those factors, and questions whether a leader is needed in the situation. That is, can a team of followers, or subordinates, in a certain situation function successfully without the guidance of a leader? In some cases, the task at hand is so clearly lined out that a leader's direction is not needed, and could be considered redundant. As with each of the other theories, they come attached with a flaw, and the flaw associated with these theories is that they are too ambiguous and not very practical in application.

Path-goal theory

Path-goal theory analyses diverse dimensions of leader behaviour such as initiating structure, consideration, authoritarianism, hierarchical influence, and closeness of supervision in terms of 'path-goal' variables such as valence and instrumentality (House, 1971). In this theory, a leader should attempt to clarify the path to a goal for a subordinate such that personal payoffs occur for a subordinate, and satisfaction and performance are increased (Keller, 1989). According to Wofford and Liska (1993) the motivational functions of the leader include: increasing personal payoffs to subordinates for work-goal attainment, clarifying the paths to these payoffs, reducing roadblocks and pitfalls that impede goal attainment, and increasing the opportunities for subordinate satisfaction. Some crucial factors that make this theory successful are: the leader must clarify and 'stick to' a goal, subordinates work together towards that goal, and an open line of communication must be present between a leader and his/her subordinates.

VDL/LMX theory

Another approach to leadership is vertical dyad linkage (VDL). This approach to leadership views leadership as an exchange relationship that develops within the vertical dyad, e.g. leader/follower relationship, over time during role-making activities (Danserau, Graen, & Haga, 1975). There are two major assumptions with this theory: members of an organisational unit who report to the same superior are sufficiently homogeneous on the relevant dimensions that they can be considered a single entity, and a superior behaves in essentially the same prescribed manner toward each of his/her members. VDL in more recent years has been altered some and renamed the leader-member exchange model (LMX). LMX is based on the concept that role-development will inherently result in differentiated role definitions and, therefore, in varied leader-member exchanges. In this LMX, the leader develops a close relationship with only a few key subordinates (Dienesch & Liden, 1986).

Transformational/transactional

The last major theory to be addressed is transformational theory (or charismatic or inspirational leadership). The basis for this theory is that leaders inspire their followers to look beyond their own interests, and to look toward a more focused or central purpose. 'Leaders who are considered transformational concentrate their efforts on longer term goals; place value and emphasis on developing and inspiring followers to pursue the vision; change or align systems to accommodate their vision rather than work within existing systems; and coach followers to take on greater responsibility for their own development, as well as the development of others' (Howell & Avolio, 1993). A theory often associated with transformational is transactional theory. Transactional is often used as a comparison to transformational in that with transactional, leaders offer their followers rewards for their performance. There is an agreement made between the leader and the follower as to what level of performance is deserving of rewards. This theory, also known as contingent reward leadership is viewed as positively linked to performance, and possibly job satisfaction. In either case, leaders must be very clear as to what the common goal is and what is expected from the followers.

Gender differences in leadership styles

There are definite trends rising between gender and leadership. The first and most overwhelming trend is the increase in opportunities for women to fill leadership roles, but there are still many obstacles for women to overcome. In an overall examination of leadership style, there are striking differences in the way women and men lead.

In the realm of leadership, men are seen as more focused on task accomplishment than maintenance of interpersonal relationships. They typically are more assertive and are motivated to master their environment. The leadership style most often adopted by men is that of an autocratic leadership where the leadership and decision making are central to the leader without

Women, in contrast, are more likely to lead with a more democratic style, involving others in leadership and decision-making. The feminine leadership model is typically characterised by cooperativeness, collaboration of managers and subordinates, lower control for the leader, and problem-solving based on intuition and empathy as well as rationality (Loden, 1985 in Eagly & Johnson, 1990).

If it is correct to assume that women and men differ in their leadership styles, a question arises of where those differences stem from. Hennig and Jardin (1987) (in Eagly & Johnson, 1990) acknowledge that sex-differentiated behaviour is closely associated with early socialisation. Does our society impose that much of an impact on our development? Perhaps we are raised open to diverse leadership styles, and once in the corporate world, we are socialised to lead in a gender-appropriate manner.

There is a difference in the leadership techniques used by men and women. Overall men are more autocratic, and women are more democratic. Who's to say which is better? One style may work best in a certain situation, but horribly in another. Shouldn't the focus be drawn from the differences in leadership style and relocated to the effectiveness of a leader in general? What does it matter if a leader uses 'feminine' or 'masculine' styles, as long as the job is done effectively? As long as there is some difference in the styles used, there will be an explosive amount of research done on the stereotypes and gender differences in leadership.

To examine the future of leadership, current issues must be addressed. Two major issues in leadership are more than likely going to set the trend for the future; gender and minority leadership issues and technological advances.

1 To address gender and minority issues in leadership, there must be some recognition that because of our gender or our race, we may approach leadership differently. It is too early to tell the effects of the diverse leadership styles, but in the next 25 years, we are

going to see an increase in both women and minorities in leadership positions. What used to be the 'good old boy' network will be replaced with a new generation of leaders. The question is who will mentor these up-and-coming leaders? If the 'good old boys' mentor them, will they in turn lead with the same styles and characteristics? Only time can tell, but leadership as we have known will face a radical change in the future.

2 Technology will have a drastic impact on leadership, as we know it. We see the rise of technological advances everyday. The computer alone revolutionised the working world, and has seen enormous changes in the last five to ten years. Imagine what 25 years will do to technology! Will the working world be strictly computers? If so, whom will leaders lead, the people who fix computers? The only restraint technology has on it is the capacity of the human mind – how quickly will it surpass that? Technological advances will change not only leadership, but also every aspect of the working world, and at the rate it is growing, it will not take 25 years before we see an incredible transformation. The past theories of leadership have sought the single 'almighty' theory. The future of leadership is becoming so diverse and broad; no single theory can address all facets of leadership. Therefore, the challenge lies in no longer explaining leadership, but observing and respecting its complexity.

Part 2

Gender and Communication Styles

Communication Enhancement Techniques

Gender and Communication Styles

Men and women operate in two very different social worlds. Men are in an ongoing contest, competing with everyone by displaying their competence and skill. Women are cautious but persistently seek intimacy; they want emotional support, cooperation, and praise. But if both sexes understand where the other is coming from, the conflicts can be reduced.

TIP BOX ♂⇨♀

MEN COMMUNICATING WITH WOMEN

A man needs to understand why women can talk to other women about a problem and yet never seem to receive any advice or criticism - because women are interacting to get support, not solutions.

Men seek to establish and maintain status and dominance while women's communicating is about rule-by-consensus. When women get together they seek the input of the other women present and make decisions based on the wishes of all. Author Deborah Tannen notes that this type of communication style is becoming more important, and is in alignment with the Japanese style of management. Men doing business with Japanese companies often have to radically change their style of communicating to accommodate the more personal and intimate approach of the Japanese businessman.

TIP BOX ♀⇨♂

WOMEN COMMUNICATING WITH MEN

A women needs to understand why men shift the topic to something they did and/or something they know about, rather than asking questions as a woman would - because asking questions might suggest the other person knows more.

Many men enjoy getting into arguments about politics, sports, or a professional issue. They enjoy the competitive process, e.g. men like their debate opponents better afterwards; women tend to like any challenger or debater less afterwards. If we fully recognise these major differences between men and women, we can understand that the man, trying to be helpful, offers the woman a solution to the problem she is sharing; she gets irritated because he seems to be assuming that he could handle the problem better than she could. Besides, his giving advice cut her off from telling all the details and her feelings! He can't understand why she becomes annoyed at him after he tries to help, and then he gets irritated with her for being a typical woman.

Women start more conversations than men, ask more questions, attempt to put the other person at ease more, are more supportive of the talker, and generally take more responsibility for the overall social situation. These are valuable, commendable skills. Men not only change the topic more but also they do 95% of the interrupting of women in mixed company!

Deborah Tannen is the author of *You Just Don't Understand: Women and Men in Conversation*. Tannen's research shows that the differences between the communication styles of men and women go far beyond mere socialisation, and appear to be inherent in the basic make up of each sex. Tannen first noticed these differences when studying videotapes another researcher had made of best friends asked to have a conversation together. In contrast to the girls, boys were extremely uncomfortable with this request. Girls in all age groups would face each other and immediately began to talk, eventually ending up discussing the problems of one girl. Boys, on the other hand, sat parallel to each other and would jump from topic to topic. Tannen observed that, 'For males, conversation is the way you negotiate your status in the group and keep people from pushing you around; you use talk to preserve your independence. Females, on the other hand, use conversation to negotiate closeness and intimacy; talk is the essence of intimacy, so being best friends means sitting and talking.'

Tannen makes the point that both sexes need to understand the inherent differences in their communication styles so that they don't expect the impossible. There is middle ground where men and women can meet and find understanding. Women must learn that the kind of intimate talk they have with their girlfriends should remain just that. Trying to turn your man into a girlfriend will usually fail because men, in general, don't create feelings of closeness in that way. Men, too can understand that when their woman is talking, she is attempting to connect to him – she's not just talking to talk, nor is she trying to readjust the status of their relationship. By sharing more of himself, he shows her, in a way she can understand, that he's not pushing her away; that he does indeed want to be close to her.

> If women speak and hear a language of connection and intimacy, while men speak and hear a language of status and independence, then communication between men and women can be like cross-cultural communication, prey to a clash of conversational styles.
>
> Deborah Tannen

Their reasons for conversing are one of the basic differences between men and women. Women tend to converse to build connections and intimacy. Life is viewed as a community and women have a need to preserve intimacy and avoid isolation. Therefore, women tend to converse about their relationships. Men perceive this often to be gossiping when in reality it is the way women build more connections and create greater levels of intimacy. Men view conversations as negotiations to obtain the upper hand. Men tend to see individuals within a hierarchy in which they are either one-up or one-down. Therefore, men converse and compare notes about things such as cars and stereo equipment. The essential element in communication for men is to gain status and independence. Another basic difference is that men give reports when they talk. Compare that to women who try to build rapport when they talk. Therefore, men give facts and information. Women are more relationship oriented. For men, talk is information. For women, talk is interaction.

TIP BOX ♂⇨♀

MEN COMMUNICATING WITH WOMEN

Ways in which a man might mistakenly invalidate feelings and perceptions or offer unwanted solutions to a woman:

- 'From now on, I'll handle it.'
- 'You shouldn't worry so much.'
- 'Why let others treat you that way? Forget them.'
- 'Why don't you just do it?'
- 'This is what you should do.'

Author, Jennifer Coates, whose studies are founded on various researches about gender specific communication, draws a similar conclusion to Deborah Tannen's when she writes: '… men pursue a style of interaction based on power, while women pursue a style based on solidarity and support'. Moreover, Jennifer Coates concludes that female communication obeys different rules from male communication, and men and women therefore have other expectations of a conversation. The sexes differ in their opinions of what constitutes a good conversation, of how conversation should progress, of how important it is to let a current speaker finish his term and of how substantial it is to support the interlocutor actively (Coates, 1986).

Questions are used more frequently by women than by men and women often employ them as a method to facilitate and maintain the flow of communication. Men, nevertheless, interpret also such questions as a request for information whereupon they like to give detailed answers, as in their eyes those who know more have a higher status. Women then often wait in vain for a question posed to them, which, from their viewpoint, would balance the conversation and indicate interrelation. Jennifer Coates writes that women make an effort to respond to what their interlocutor has said before and then forge links to a similar topic. Men tend to ignore what has been said before and mainly concentrate on making their own point. They want to talk about what is in their interest, no matter whether there is a link to the previous subject of discussion. This observation, too, reflects Deborah Tannen's theory. Women show more interest in each other in order to improve their relationships, men preserve their independence by not feeling obliged to respond to the previous topic and claim their status by contributing as many of their own points of interest as possible to keep the conversation going as they wish (Coates, 1986).

According to Jennifer Coates, women intend the opposite with interruptions. They want to show that they are actively listening and support the person they are listening to. While their interlocutor speaks, women often throw in short comments, nod and currently use minimal responses such as 'hmm'. Such signals of active listenership are used much less frequently by men. If men interrupt, they mostly intend to take the turn, which implies that the current speaker cannot finish her/his turn. As a consequence in mixed-sex conversations, women often feel they are not being respected, speak less than men and are hurt as such behaviour violates the rules of their co-operatively organised conversational style (Coates, 1986).

But men do not mean such interruptions personally, they are a part of their competitive way of communicating. Deborah Tannen justifies men's behaviour in the following way: 'But the result that men do most of the talking does not necessarily mean that men intend to prevent women from speaking. Those who readily speak up assume that others are as free as they are to take the floor' (Tannen, 1992). So men are often astonished when women get more and more silent in a conversation which in their eyes is unfair because it makes them think women lack participation and do not use their right to interrupt a man and take the floor themselves. Men sometimes do not understand that what for them forms a natural part of conversation would make women feel rough and unfriendly. Jennifer Coates concludes that women are much more concerned to facilitate conversation than men, who are more concerned to say a lot themselves.

TIP BOX ♀⇨♂

WOMEN COMMUNICATING WITH MEN

Ways in which a woman might unknowingly annoy a man by offering advice or seemingly harmless criticism:

- 'You're not leaving yourself much time.'
- 'You shouldn't work so hard.'
- 'Your office is a mess. How can you think in here?'
- 'Don't put it there. It will get lost.'

According to Jennifer Coates, women talking together reveal a lot from their private lives, above all their feelings and their relationships. They stick to one topic for a long time, let all speakers finish their terms, make an effort to have everybody participate in the discussion and want to avoid a situation where somebody dominates. Men, when relating together, scarcely talk about themselves, but 'compete to prove themselves better informed about current affairs, travel, sport, etc.' They change topic very often, everyone seeks to dominate the conversation and 'over time establish a reasonably stable hierarchy, with some men dominating conversation and others talking very little' (Coates, 1986).

If men dominate women in a conversation they seldom do it on purpose, it rather happens because communication is a means to mutual challenge for them. Women consequently often feel restricted by men's more aggressive conversational style and thus get frustrated and speak less. In such situations where women get silent men may feel that their female interlocutor leaves the talking to them or has not got much to say. Men's conversational priorities are to achieve their aims and remain independent. But they pay less attention on whether their more aggressive way of talking puts their relationships to their fellow beings at risk. Women, however, put up with not achieving their goals or achieving them less quickly if they in return for it can establish and maintain relationships and intimacy. The distinct conversational styles reflect the different needs the sexes have and show that women have other focal points in life than men. One should look upon this as natural and realise that both styles have advantages and disadvantages. The two styles should be regarded as equal and although the sexes might learn from each other's styles it would be unrealistic and wrong to adjust them to each other.

Creating closeness

Women create feelings of closeness by conversing. Men don't use communication in this way, so they can't figure out why women continually talk. Tannen notes that men are confused by the various ways women use conversation to be intimate with others. One of these ways she calls 'troubles talk.' She says, 'For women, talking about troubles is the essence of connection. I tell you my troubles, you tell me your troubles, and we're close. Men, however, hear troubles talk as a request for advice, so they respond with a solution.' When a man offers this kind of information, the woman often feels as if he is trying to diminish her problem or cut her off. In his eyes, he's being supportive, because men don't talk to each other about their troubles unless they really do want a solution; talking about their problems is wallowing in them. The man doesn't realise that the woman was simply trying to establish a certain kind of intimacy with him – inviting him to reciprocate and share himself with her.

Hundreds of years ago, when the Japanese first started training the Samurai Warriors, they trained women as well as men. And women were just as accurate as the men. But they had to stop including women because they were being killed much more often. Why? Because they would hold back and attack only when they were 100% certain that that enemy meant them harm. They couldn't be 100% certain until the sword was already in their bellies! So women were being killed much more often than men, despite the fact that they were just as accurate with their weapons.

Problem solving

Men tend to talk less about problems than women, as they look upon problems as a sign of weakness and being weak from their outlook equals having a low status. Women, nevertheless, regard discussing problems as a good way to establish intimacy and reinforce relationships. When a discussion comes up to problems, the two sexes react correspondingly differently. Women make an effort to show concern and sympathy and often contribute their own similar experiences, but men straightforwardly seek for solutions and want to give useful advice. In mixed-sex conversations, this can possibly lead to frustrations for both parties. As men expect to hear solutions to their problems, they feel it is illogical and even lowering if a woman's reaction is sympathy. Women, on the other hand, often feel hurt if a man does not show concern for their problems by showing sympathy but responding with a concrete solution or a piece of advice.

Women like to discuss problems as a way of building intimacy and connection. Men like to solve problems. Remember, men have conversations to obtain the upper hand; therefore, giving advice comes naturally. Women, on the other hand, have conversations to build closeness; therefore, giving empathy comes naturally. Men need to achieve results and like to work out the details of solving a problem alone. To offer a man unsolicited advice is to presume that he doesn't know what to do or that he can't do it on his own. When a woman is asking a man for support, she needs to be direct and brief. She needs to avoid using blame language. She'll find a man wants to make improvements when he feels he is being approached as the solution to a problem rather than as the problem itself.

A woman's sense of self is defined through her feelings and the quality of her relationships. To feel better, women get together and openly talk about their problems. Women talking together doesn't always need to produce solutions. A woman under stress is not immediately concerned with finding solutions to her problems but rather seeks relief by expressing herself and being understood. She is fulfilled through talking about the details of her problem. Conflicts will tend to escalate when a man begins to invalidate a woman's feelings and she responds to him disapprovingly. Women too can cover up their real emotion. For example, they may use concern and worry as a way of avoiding anger, guilt and fear or they may use fear as a way of avoiding anger and sadness.

Women tend to:

- seek intimacy and rapport through their verbal conversations.
  Consequently, at work they tend to ask for others opinions and look for consensus. Men can interpret this as being uncertain and indecisive, diminishing women's perceived authority.
- downplay their authority, assuming that if people know they're the boss why lord it over them.
  While this tends to work well with other women, they make themselves vulnerable to a man challenging them and taking some of their authority. Women need to assess in what situations they may need to assert their authority.

Men tend to:

- have a conversational style of banter and opposition, which helps them, maintain their status in a conversation.
  This style inhibits some men and many women who tend to clam up and not say much. If men want the input of all their colleagues, they may need to evaluate when this style is and isn't effective.

- practice 'public' speaking while women practice 'private speaking.'
  In a meeting, this means a man may feel more comfortable taking the floor and asserting his ideas. Women need to be prepared to jump into the meeting early and make several suggestions to increase their visibility.
- interrupt women more than they interrupt men, or than women interrupt either men or women.
  When they do this, they diminish the woman's power.
- want to maintain their status and perceive asking questions as going 'one down.'
  Consequently, they sometimes act without all the information, or are prevented from acting because they don't have the information they need.
- solve or fix problems when they hear about them.
  A woman, who may only be talking about a problem to build rapport, doesn't feel that he is listening to her. Men need to try listening to a woman with the goal of understanding her, not fixing the situation.

How people communicate is deeply tied to who they think they are. Therefore, it isn't easy to change one's style. Men feel less powerful and vulnerable when they use women's styles. Women often feel they are mean or rude when they adopt men's styles. The secret is for all of us to become bilingual and use the style that is most appropriate to the situation.

A study was conducted at Valdosta State University in Georgia, US, 1998, to determine students' perceptions of gender differences in several areas of non-verbal communication. Specifically, the areas of eye contact, gestures, smiles, personal space, touch, and interpretation of non-verbal cues were examined. The results were:

- **When asked who touches more,** 57.8 percent of female respondents agreed that they touch others more than a male does. However, the experts had mixed opinions on the subject. Hanna and Wilson (1998) felt that women touch others less than men do. But Burgoon, Buller, and Woodall (1996) conclude that women give and receive more touches than men (except when initiating courtship). They explain how touch is considered a feminine-appropriate behaviour and a masculine-inappropriate one. Mothers touch female infants more than male infants, and female children desire and offer more non-aggressive touch than male children. Another important point made by Burgoon, Buller, and Woodall is that touch initiation may depend not on gender alone but also on the internationality of the touch, the age and relationship of the participants, and the setting where the touch occurs.

- **Which gender was able to interpret non-verbal cues better?** Of the female respondents, 73.7 percent agreed that they could interpret another person's non-verbals better than a male. From the review of literature, all experts agreed that, in fact, females are better interpreters of non-verbals. Burgoon, Buller, and Woodall (1996) described women as being more sensitive communicators. And Ivy and Backlund (1994) conclude that women more actively communicate the importance of relationships by using a number of verbal and non-verbal channels.

- **Who used more gestures?** The majority of the females surveyed (74.5 percent) felt that they typically use more gestures than a male. However, the opinions of experts in literature were mixed. For instance, Hanna and Wilson (1998) felt that women used fewer gestures than men. These authors also stated that women use fewer gestures when they are with other women but more gestures with men. However, Burgoon, Buller, and Woodall (1996) felt that the difference was in the types of gestures used rather than in the frequency of use. A very large majority of the female respondents (83.7 percent) felt that they typically smile more often than a male does. However, almost everyone surveyed said they would automatically return a smile if someone smiled at them first.

- **Who required more personal space?** Fifty-six percent of the female respondents felt they require more personal space than a male. However, all the experts in literature agreed that males used more personal space than females.

- **Who established more eye contact?** The females surveyed thought they do; 67.5 percent agreed that females typically establish more eye contact than men do. Burgoon, Buller, and Woodall (1996) concluded that North American women engage in more eye contact during conversations than men. Ivy and Backlund (1994) suggested that women (more often in a subordinate role) make more eye contact than a person in a dominant position. In addition, Ivy and Backlund found that women were more comfortable giving eye contact than men (1994).

Body language of the genders

Men:

- are not as sensitive to the communication cues of others
- tend to approach women more closely in terms of their personal space
- take up more physical space when sitting or standing, with arms and legs stretched out away from their body
- tend to cock their head to the side and look at the other person from an angle when listening
- provide fewer facial expressions in feedback and fewer reactions
- tend to display frowning and squinting when listening
- stare more in negative interaction
- gesture away from the body
- assume more reclined positions when sitting and lean backward when listening.

Women:

- display smiling and head-nodding when listening
- lower their eyes more to avert gaze in negative interaction
- take up less physical space, sitting with arms and legs toward their body
- do not approach men as closely in terms of their personal space

- tend to look at the other person directly facing them with their head and eyes facing forward when listening
- provide more facial expressions and more reactions
- gesture toward the body
- assume more forward positions when sitting and lean forward when listening
- have greater sensitivity and acuity toward other people's non-verbal communication cues.

Genderflex

Judith Tingley PhD is a psychologist and business communication consultant who has studied the problem of gender differences in communication. She devised the term, Genderflex. Genderflex is a term to describe temporary shifts in communication behaviour between the sexes. Genderflex is often used to increase an individual's potential for influence. Genderflex occurs when a man temporarily uses speech patterns or sentence structures that are typically used by females, or vice versa. Dr Tingley identifies content, style, and structure as three important gender-specific communication differences. Content simply refers to the difference in topics of discussion between males and females. The second difference, communication style, reveals the difference in thought processes between men and women. When confronted with a problem, men are likely to search for an answer, while women search to find an understanding to the problem. Finally, sentence structure differences show a wide gap between men and women. Male communication tends to be less descriptive and to the point, while female communication is often detailed, apologetic, and vague.

TIP BOX ♀⇨♂

WOMEN COMMUNICATING WITH MEN

Women tend to be more resistant to adapting to communication styles; therefore, both sides must adapt to each other to be successful in communicating. These adaptations will result in stronger communication skills. Women should continue to use facilitative listening skills, add sports, money, and business to her lingo but need to avoid using vague terms, excessive amounts of words, apologies, and disclaimers.

American Management Association

Speech patterns

There are some specific ways in which men and women's speech patterns differ from each other. Women are more hesitant in communication when asked a question. Women respond with a tentative style of speech that reduces the meaning of the words they speak. This results in the women appearing less intelligent and knowledgeable. Men, on the other hand, tend to dominate the conversations in which they are involved.

Although speech patterns reveal some of the ways in which women can weaken their impact, another way that men and women reveal their speech differences is through speech content. An example of differences in content includes the use of emotional verbs. Women are more apt to use emotional verbs such as 'I love . . . I feel . . . or I hope.' Another example in content differences is the use of qualifiers or quantifiers. Men are much more likely to use quantifier words such as 'always,' 'never,' 'all,' or 'none,' whereas women typically use qualifier words such as 'a bit' or 'kind of.' The result is that quantifier words produce a more confident tone than do qualifier words (Schrank).

Men tend to:

- make more declarative statements, e.g. 'That was a good meeting.'
- use more interjections when changing topics, e.g. 'Oh', 'Listen!'
- ask fewer questions to stimulate conversation
- rarely discuss their personal life in business
- speak in a louder voice
- use loudness to emphasise points
- sound more monotonous in speech – they use approximately 3 tones when talking
- interrupt others more and allow fewer interruptions
- disclose less personal information about themselves
- make direct accusations, e.g. 'Your presentation skills aren't too good.'
- make more direct statements
- use less intensifiers.

Women's language

Robin Lakoff was one of the first women to publish theories on the existence of women's language. Her book *Language and Woman's Place* (1975) and her article entitled *'Woman's Language'* have served as the basis for much research on the subject. In her 1975 article, she published ten basic assumptions about what she felt constituted a special women's language.

Special lexicon:	Women use more words for things.
Upward inflection:	This is a rising intonation at the end of a sentence. The inflection provides the listener with a sense of uncertainty. Although you cannot hear the inflection by reading the following sentence, try speaking it out loud to notice the inflection: 'My computer was down yesterday, so I didn't complete the report?'
Disclaimer:	This is a phrase at the beginning of a sentence

	that weakens the remaining information. Sentences that begin with 'I think that . . .' provide an excellent example of the use of a disclaimer in speech.
Hedges:	The hedge is very similar to a disclaimer, but it is usually not placed at the beginning of a sentence. The inclusion of phases like 'maybe' and 'sort of' are examples of a hedge.
(Super) polite forms:	'Would you mind...' 'I'd appreciate it if ...'
Tag endings:	Tag endings, occur when a question is 'tagged' on to the end of a sentence. The result is that the speaker appears unsure of her thoughts. A good example would be the following comment: 'This is a hard project, isn't it?'
Speaking in italics:	Intonational emphasis equal to underlining words – so, very, quite.
Empty adjectives:	Divine, lovely, adorable, etc.
Hypercorrect grammar and pronunciation:	English class grammar and clear enunciation.
Sense of humour: lacking:	Women do not tell jokes well and often don't understand the punchline of jokes.
Direct quotation:	Men paraphrase more often.

Women tend to:

- use more intensifiers such as 'few', 'so', 'really', 'much', 'quite'
- make more tentative statements and use 'tag endings' or upward inflections which make statements sound like questions, e.g. 'It's a nice day, isn't it?'
- use more conjunctions when changing topics, e.g. 'and', 'but', 'however'
- ask more questions to stimulate conversations
- tend to establish more business relationships through discussing their personal life

- speak in a softer voice
- use pitch and inflection to emphasise points
- sound more emotional in speech – they use approximately five tones when talking
- interrupt others less and allow more interruptions
- disclose more personal information about themselves
- make more indirect accusations – they use 'why', which sounds like nagging, e.g. 'Why don't you ever get a report in on time?'
- make more indirect statements.

TIP BOX ♂⇨♀

MEN COMMUNICATING WITH WOMEN

Men have a natural competitive style that may make them resistant to adapting to women's communication styles. Men should continue to use a precise and concise structure of communication. Males should add people, feelings, and relationships to their communication infrastructure. Men should also learn to use people-related stories when engaging in casual conversation with women.

American Management Association

Seven important questions

Is assertiveness in women viewed negatively by others?

- Research has suggested that the adoption of task behaviours (a focus on getting things done) enhances a female's adaptability in the organisation (but the adoption of relationship behaviours – focusing on the relationships among people – proves problematic for males). 'The healthiest and best-liked individuals, male or female, were assertive, decisive, and intellectual, rather than nurturant, responsive and emotional'(Fitzpatrick). Therefore, women may want to focus on task- and impression-management goals in their interactions.

- Subordinates prefer a supervisor to balance a task-orientated style with a relationship-oriented style.

Who interrupts the most?

- Some of the interruptions that women experience come from other women. Women, when they do interrupt, are more likely to interrupt other women than they are to interrupt men, according to studies.
- Women are more likely than men to allow an interruption of their talk to be successful (they do not resist the interruption as much as men do).
- Men are more likely than women to interrupt the speaking of other people.

What are the gender patterns in informal group meetings?

- When the floor is an informal, collaborative venture, women display a fuller range of language ability. Here, in the kind of conversation where women excel, people jointly build an idea, operate on the same wavelengths, and have deep conversational overlaps.

What are some of the ways women are affected by these communication patterns?

- Many women feel inhibited in formal, mixed-gender groups.
- Some women participate in creating their own passive participation – by allowing interruptions, by not taking advantage of natural pauses in the conversation, or by asking questions without explaining the context out of which the question emerged.
- Some women, when they do gain the floor, talk too fast as though they know they are about to be interrupted.
- When a woman is interrupted often or her comments are ignored, she may come to believe that what she has to say must not be important.
- Women are less likely than men to have confidence in their ability to make persuasive arguments.

Are gender differences in communication patterns related to power?

- Differences are linked to power, and are context-specific. Differences are socially created and therefore may be socially altered.
- Studies have found that talking time is related both to gender (because men spend more time talking than women) and to organisational power (because the more powerful spend more time talking than the less powerful).
- When people are strangers, they expect less competence from women than from men.
- But if women are known to have prior experience or expertise related to the task, or if women are assigned leadership roles, then women show greatly increased verbal behaviours in mixed-sex groups.

Who talks the most?

- In one experiment, the men with expertise talked longer than the women with expertise.
- Men initiate more interaction than do women.
- In mixed-gender groups, at public gatherings, and in many informal conversations, men spend more time talking than do women.

What about gender patterns in formal group meetings?

- When women do ask a question, they take less time in asking it than do men. In addition, they employ much less pre-question predication, they are less likely to ask multiple questions, and they are more likely than men to phrase their question in personal terms.
- In meetings, men gain the floor more often, and keep the floor for longer periods of time, regardless of their status in the organisation.
- In professional conferences, women take a less active part in responding to papers.

TIP BOX ♀⇆♂

MEN AND WOMEN COMMUNICATING WITH EACH OTHER

Dr. Tingley suggests using a six-step process to adapt to gender differences in communication.

1. Adjust your attitude and open your mind to the idea of communicating in a different manner than you are accustomed to. Individuals must be willing to accept the differences as normal, expected and positive.
2. Acknowledge that there are differences in communication styles. Both sexes must develop an objective, non-judgemental awareness of differences in communication. This will help to put them in the right frame of mind to communicate with the opposite sex.
3. Assess differences without using judgement. Individuals must communicate that they have identified a difference regardless of whether it is in content, style or structure.
4. Be willing to adjust your attitude again. The final resistance to change should be used as a motivator for adaptive communication techniques.
5. Choose techniques for action or response. Make sure that the necessary adaptations are made to improve communication.
6. Generalise from the specific. If a positive response occurs from the previous five suggestions, then an individual needs to assess the technique used, and apply the findings to similar situations.

Communication Enhancement Techniques

How do we increase the effectiveness of our communication with the opposite sex? Similar to most diversity issues, the solution lies primarily in awareness and understanding. Becoming familiar with the many differences between men and women, and understanding that these differences are desirable and arbitrary, not right or wrong, will diminish the majority of communication problems. Recognising how our own behaviour and language styles differ, thereby triggering misperceptions and misunderstandings by the opposite sex, goes a long way toward improving communication.

Body language

According to a University of Southern California study, up to 55% of influence in communication comes from your body language. So how can you can control it? First, you must understand that you can control your emotions by controlling your physiology. Some people say that they cannot seem to feel good no matter how much they tell themselves to feel good. The experts tell you when you start out to increase your confidence, that you must 'fake it till you make it'. What they are trying to tell you is, move your body as if you already know what you are doing, and your brain will begin to believe you do in fact know what you are doing.

The first person you need to impact with positive body language is not others, but rather yourself. If you cannot influence yourself to change your emotional state of being, how can you impact others? Start by controlling your breath. Experiment with taking deep breaths from the diaphragm. The fastest way to change your mental state and body language is to change your breathing. Your mind will follow the lead you dictate for your body and your life. Start by deciding to control your body language in order to feel better about yourself. Over time, others will begin to feel better about themselves while they are around you, because they are unconsciously mirroring or emulating you.

Using body language is an unspoken but vital part of communication. People-skills are all about reading the verbal and the non-verbal. Body language can say what words can't. It can show you where there are contradictions in words. It can provide encouragement.

Actions speak louder than words – meaning how we communicate with our body is often in conflict with what we verbally say. We give away non-verbal signals through our gestures, facial expression, eyes, body movements and verbal language. Verbal language, in this context, doesn't so much mean what you say as how you say it and key words you use such as 'You must ...' as opposed to 'I would appreciate it if you could ...'

'Leakage' are the clues that give away your feelings via verbal and non-verbal language despite your attempts to control them, such as:

- fiddling which conveys nerves, tapping indicates, impatience or anger
- changes in pitch and tone, which can signal timidness (correct breathing and relaxation will help you project your voice assertively)
- a clenched jaw indicating tension or aggression (watch for the automatic smile that says, 'please don't be angry').

> Practising T'ai Chi, Alexander Technique, yoga and other forms of postural exercise and meditation can give you an upright, relaxed and balanced posture which in turn will give you internal confidence.

Going by appearance

You make an impression during the first three minutes of entering a room. Dress, appearance and grooming combine to give other people an instant visual image of who you are.

Using touch

A person's handshake can tell you about their attitude. Do you recognise the limp handshake, the soggy palm routine, and the hand crusher? What initial impression do you form about people with certain handshakes?

The right proximity

The more formal the relationship, the further away we tend to stand from each other. As a relationship develops, so the space between decreases. Physical barriers such as desks or podiums also represent proximity (or lack of it).

Watching the face

Anger can make someone go red or white. Red tends to indicate a more apparent anger whereas someone who has gone white with anger is more unpredictable. Eye contact is vital in imparting a sense of confidence and trustworthiness. Glaring may indicate anger while evasive eye action could indicate dishonesty or shyness. The more intimately we know a person, the further down their body our gaze goes. With business acquaintances, we tend to look in a t-shape, across the eyes and down to the mouth. Be aware of smiling to appease anger in someone else or having a fixed smile born out of sheer nerves.

Hand gestures

Someone waving their hands around can be trying to distract you from what they are saying. If you are a woman in male company and the man runs his hand down his tie, this could mean he is attracted to you! Touching the nose or mouth while speaking may indicate that you're not telling the truth while touching the ear could show that you're not sure about what you are hearing.

Body stance

Crossed arms and legs indicate a closed mind while an open body shows an open mind. When you are sitting down with someone and their legs are crossed towards you, they're interested in what you have to say. If you are standing with your feet directed towards the person you are with, you are showing friendliness.

Behavioural styles

People-skills involve a set of behavioural styles. Below are four categories of behaviours.

Which behavioural style are you?

Groupie	Doer	Thinker	Creator
accessible	aggressive	cautious	ambitious
adaptable	assertive	concise	creative
caring	competitive	conscientious	curious
calm	confident	dedicated	dramatic
courteous	decisive	dependable	excitable
diplomatic	determined	efficient	extrovert
discreet	dynamic	enquiring	flexible
easy going	energetic	fussy	humorous
empathic	enterprising	impartial	imaginative
encouraging	firm	logical	innovative
fair	initiator	methodical	intuitive
friendly	leader	meticulous	inventive
helpful	hardworking	objective	lateral thinker
likeable	practical	ordered	visionary
outgoing	pro-active	organised	
perceptive	resourceful	patient	
persuasive	strong-willed	precise	

Groupies

A Groupie is someone who needs to relate in order to get a sense of self. They enjoy interaction and find other people reassuring. When relating to a Groupie:

- find some area of common ground
- be responsive to their contributions.

Doers

Doers need to get results. They seldom involve themselves in idle chitchat and want to get on with the job. When interacting with a Doer:

- deal in facts
- be specific.

Thinkers

Thinkers will deal in facts and logic. They are likely to be cautious and lean towards perfectionism. When communicating with a Thinker:

- be accurate
- produce practical evidence.

Creators

Creators are instinctive and creative with a low threshold of boredom. When relating to a Creator:

- be stimulating and fun
- provide extra angles to work with.

Reading the voice

If a person is tense, his or her voice might be high or fast. Anger might reflect in a harsh voice that wants to over-ride everyone else's. Someone who is shy or doubtful might come across as monotonic (a droning sound all in one tone), mumbled or stuttering.

The emphasis you give words can alter the meaning of a sentence:

Are you coming to the meeting?
- This implies a level of disbelief.

Are ***you*** coming to the meeting?
- This suggests the questioner wants to know if that person in particular is coming to the meeting.

Are you ***coming*** to the meeting?
- This implies a questioning of an action.

Are you coming to the ***meeting***?
- This suggests impatience.

You need to be aware of the level at which you are pitching your language.

Mirroring another person

Mirroring is the art of matching some of your behaviours to that of the other person in order to get into their world. It is possible to match body stance, facial expressions, voice tone, pitch and volume, gestures, eye contact, verbal behaviour and even the breathing.

> **The Mirroring & Matching Technique**
>
> Mirror the physiology of people you wish to influence. If they are down, go down to their level. If they are up, come up to their level. If they are talking fast, you talk fast. If they are slouching, you slouch. Then, as you are talking with them, slowly begin to make small changes in your body. Your goal is to bring the person you are trying to influence into the physiology that will be most effective for getting your end outcome, and you want the other party to feel good about themselves, about you, and about being with you.

Assertive? Aggressive? Passive?

Assertiveness is directly telling someone what you want and negotiating with them for a mutually satisfying outcome. It is about being open and standing up for your rights while realising that other people share those same rights. An assertive person has a strong sense of personal power and confidence. An assertive person is someone who is aware of their own thoughts, feelings and behaviours and they take responsibility for themselves.

Recognising the victim

Victims are those who believes that everything that happens to them is the fault of someone else. They have abdicated personal responsibility and behave as if they have no control over what happens to them. Victims feel helpless and powerless and will allow other people to define them and control their personal space.

Recognising the aggressor

Aggressors are people who are dominant and need to be in control. They come over as loud and large. Someone who is aggressive is often hiding someone who is frightened of feeling vulnerable. An aggressor will invade another person's personal space in an effort to control him or her before being controlled. Aggressors would feel as if other people are there for their purpose.

Using the 'I' word

When we converse with someone, we often use another person to express our own thoughts or feelings 'they always say it's better to give than receive', or 'he made me really angry'. In reality we are saying, 'I think it is better to give than to receive' and 'I feel really angry'. There are two ways to use the 'I' statement. The first is in a self-centred way 'I want, I feel, I will'. The unspoken words are 'I don't give a monkey's what the rest of you think, feel or want'. The second is the assertive and confident way of using it, 'I feel uncomfortable about this situation, how do you feel?'. The second way is owning the feelings and also respecting the rights of others to have feelings.

Use 'I' when disclosing feelings, thoughts and actions. You are showing responsibility for owning them and also acknowledging your separateness to another. This approach will engender less defensiveness in someone else.

Negative assertion

It is possible to gain personal understanding about ourselves if we use a technique called Negative Assertion. This is where we assertively accept something, which is negative about ourselves by understanding that a mistake is only a mistake. A criticism does not imply we are a worthless human being. It suggests that a particular behaviour or attitude is not helpful to us. But it is our responsibility to determine whether or not the criticism is valid, either in part or in whole. The idea is to accept the problem and focus on what is to be done about it.

Negative inquiry

You could use this technique to prompt further criticism about yourself by asking for more information, about yourself or your behaviour. Someone may say to you, 'I'm not sure your management style would suit the new team.' Your reply could be, 'How do you see my management style at the moment?'

Further tips in dealing with criticism include:

- developing problem-solving skills
- assessing whether the criticism is really worth following up
- asking for time and coming back to the person
- clearing up any misunderstandings.

How do you come across?

	AGGRESSIVE	PASSIVE	ASSERTIVE
VOICE	firm, sarcastic, loud, hard, sharp, strident	wobbly, whining, monotonic, quiet	steady, firm, clear, controlled
SPEECH	abrupt, fast, clipped	hesitant, jerky, throat swallowing	fluent, steady, emphasising key words
FACE	scowling, chin forward	ghost smile, quick changing features	open, non-verbal and verbal agreement
EYES	staring, slit	looking down, evasive	firm, direct
GESTURES	finger pointing or stabbing or thumping	hand wringing, covering mouth, fiddling	open hands
BODY	striding round, invasive of body space	hunched shoulders, steps back, arms crossed, feet shuffling	sits/stands upright, head up
VERBAL	excessive use of 'I', boasting, threatening, put downs, sarcasm, blame, ignoring response, interrupting	rambling, self put downs, apologetic, justification, allowing interruptions	brief, clear, direct, problem solving questions, constructive criticism, negotiation

Being positive

- Isolate destructive words such as 'only' and 'just'.
- Take mental control and turn the negative messages into positive ones.
- Accentuate the positive.
- Change to an active and problem solving framework.
- Identify positive role models.
- Learn to like who you are.

Assertive behaviour is -

smiling	proximity
relaxed tone of voice	clear voice
sounding sincere	controlled
fluent	emphasising key words
relaxed jaw	firm
direct	brief statements
problem solving	using questions
constructive criticism	sharing

Passive behaviour (traditionally women's behaviour) is -

excessive apologies	hedging, e.g. perhaps
fillers e.g. um, well, y'know	powerless voice
self-effacing remarks	tag questions, e.g. aren't I right?
avoiding eye contact	allowing the invasion of personal space
handwashing	meek tone of voice
allowing interruptions	talking little
talking quietly	whining
monotonic voice	hesitance
jerky speech	throat swallowing
lip licking	ghost smile
being evasive	fiddling
feet shuffling	covering mouth with hand
stepping back	rambling

disclaimers, e.g. I'm probably wrong but -

Aggressive/controlling behaviour (traditionally men's behaviour) is -

harsh tone of voice	set mouth
staring eyes	interrupting
talking loudly	talking quickly
ignoring responses	stabbing fingers
sarcasm	shouting
abrupt tone	fist thumping
striding round	crossing arms
threatening questions	using 'shoulds and oughts'
using put downs	boastfulness
being opinionated	ignoring other people's feelings

Critical thinking

'Critical thinking is the art of thinking about your thinking while you are thinking in order to make your thinking better.' Such thinking involves working with the basic element of thought such as point of view, purpose, information, question, assumption, implications, interpretation and concepts and assessing these elements using intellectual criteria such as clarity, logic, accuracy, breadth, precision, relevance, and depth.

Critical thinking gets us involved in a dialogue with the ideas we hear so that we can summarise, analyse, hypothesise and evaluate the ideas we encounter. While there are a number of excellent resources on the topic of critical thinking, among them Jan Rehner's *Practical Strategies for Critical Thinking* and Vincent Ruggierio's *Becoming a Critical Thinker*, the most important thing to know about critical thinking is that it can be developed and mastered with time and practice.

One of the best things you can do to develop your ability to think critically is to become conscious of applying a series of questions. While there are a limitless number of possible questions to ask, it is possible to categorise the questions you come up with into groups that represent the level of thinking the questions make you do. The four levels of questions include: summary/definition, analysis, hypothesis and evaluation. These capture the variety of questions that we can ask. The purpose of developing these categories is to give us a rough guide so that we can choose what questions to ask for the level of thinking that we want to do. Below are listed some example question frames in each of the question type categories:

Examples of evaluation questions:

... effective or ineffective ...?
... relevant or irrelevant ...?
... applicable or not applicable ...?
... proven or not proven...?
what are the advantages/disadvantages of ...?
what are the pros or cons of ...?
what should or should not happen ...?
what is my opinion ...?

Examples of summary and definition questions:

what is ...?
what is an example of ...?

Examples of analysis questions:

why ...?
what are the reasons for ...?
what other examples of ...?
what are the causes/results of ...?
what is the relationship between ... and ...?
what is (are) the problems or conflicts or issues ...?

Examples of hypothesis questions:

if ... had happened, then what would be different ...?
if ... occurs, then what happens ...?

Additional skills useful for developing critical thinking include:

Problem solving	to analyse alternatives
Understanding how we learn	to create environments to gather data based on our understanding of ourselves
Creativity	to develop lateral perceptions and to translate them into critical reality
Decision making	to gather, evaluate and act
Mindpower, e.g. memorising	to use mind techniques for logical analysis
Planning	to identify courses of action based on criteria, to set goals, implement and review

Listening skills

Poor listening equates to misunderstandings and time wasting errors. It leads to lower productivity and lower morale. Most of us think we are good listeners. We spend up to 80% of our working hours either listening or acting on what we hear. Untrained listeners lose 75% of what they hear in a matter of hours and often capture less than half of the message at the time they receive it.

Do you hear or do you listen? What is the difference? We can all hear unless we have an impairment of some sort, but listening is more sophisticated. You could hear a work colleague say 'I can't complete this project by the deadline'. But if you listened to their tone of voice, how they said the words and their body language, you might pick up how worried they are about not meeting their commitment or how they're not asking for help when they need it. So instead of thinking, well here's someone who can't get their act together and finish something on time, you might consider sitting down with them and asking what the problem is or how could you could help them.

There can be many sources of interference in you as a listener such as:

- when the values you support are under attack
- when you don't feel accepted by speaker

- when an apology from you should be forthcoming
- when you have to admit an error
- when you have heard the discourse before
- when you can't wait to say something
- when the person speaks with a dialect or accent
- if there is anger and other extreme emotions
- with hearing difficulties
- with sight difficulties
- with physical distractions, fatigue or illness
- when there is a low attention span
- when there are time pressures
- if you doubt the trustworthiness of the speaker
- through excessive daydreaming
- if there is a perceived lack of relevance
- with memory difficulties
- where there is limited vocabulary
- given a sensitive topic area
- when feeling threatened
- where there is anxiety and tension
- where personal need results in selective listening
- if there are areas of prejudice
- where you have a dislike of a person
- when you cannot remove persistent thoughts
- if the needs of another demand involvement by you
- if the appearance of the speaker is extreme.

Others might find it difficult to listen to you when:

- you ramble and go off the subject
- you speak for too long
- you exaggerate in your approach or the facts
- you make too many points
- you do not concentrate on your listener
- you become dogmatic
- you are not sure of what you are trying to say

Some key points for good listening include:

- not letting your biases prevent you from seeing other points of view

- asking open-ended questions to expand on information exchange
- learning the physical and verbal skills that make you look open
- testing your ability to question for content and intent of the speaker
- using listening to build relationships and determine needs of others
- understanding your own listening style and develop an awareness of the listening needs of others
- avoiding or ignore distractions
- maintaining eye contact
- evaluating the message, not the speaker
- not interrupting
- not dwelling on one fragment of a message
- not jumping to conclusions but hearing the person out
- not thinking of things not related to the subject at hand
- using interjections such as 'yes' or 'go on'
- focusing on what is being said

Using effective questioning

If you couldn't ask a question, how would you know an answer? We ask ourselves questions. We ask questions of others. It's how we find things out. Questioning helps to clarify and focus our thoughts and actions. There are several types of questioning techniques:

Closed questions	Closed questions restrict the response of the other person. For example, 'Did you think the report was useful?' is closed while, 'What did you think of the report?' is open and widens the response out.
Specification questions	These types of questions focus in on the details of the problem, such as, 'When you say he keeps badgering you, what exactly do you mean?'
Elaboration questions	Ones that give another the chance to expand what they're talking about including, 'What else would you like to tell me?'

Personal responsibility questions	These imply that others have the responsibility for owning a problem and for making choices that contributes to solving it. Typical question-types include, 'What skills might you develop in order to help you with this problem?'
Leading questions	Ones that put the answer in the other person's mouth such as, 'She really gets up your nose doesn't she?
Feeling questions	These questions elicit feelings generated by a problem and might include, 'How do you feel about that?'

Examples of powerful questions to ask

- 'What would you be willing to give up for that?'
- 'If you could change one thing, what would it be?'
- 'What have you learned?'
- 'How important is this?'
- 'Where do you feel stuck?'
- 'What can we do for you?'
- 'What do you think the problem is?'
- 'What's your role in this issue?'
- 'What have you tried so far? What worked? What didn't?'
- 'What can you do for yourself?'
- 'Have you experienced anything like this before? (If so, what did you do?)'
- 'What's preventing you from ...?'

In order to co-ordinate our life and work with the lives and work of other people, we all need to know more of what other people are feeling and thinking, wanting and planning. But our usual 'yes/no' questions actually tend to shut people up rather than open them up. You can encourage your conversation partners to share more of their thoughts and feelings by asking 'open-ended' rather than 'yes/no' questions. Open-ended questions allow for a wide range of responses. For example, asking, 'What did you think of the conference?' will evoke a more detailed response than, 'Did you like the conference?'

which could be answered with a yes or no.

Even if our goal is to persuade, we can't do a good job of that unless we address our listener's concerns, and we won't understand those concerns unless we ask questions that invite discussion. When you are under time pressure, it is tempting to push people to make yes-no decisions. Here are some examples of open-ended questions that could be helpful in solving problems in a way that meets more of everyone's needs.

- 'What do you think about moving the office to Scarborough?' (rather than 'Is it OK with you if we ... ?')
- 'How are you feeling about all of this?'
- 'How ready are you to ... ?' (rather than 'Are you ready to ...?')
- 'How comfortable are you with Plan D?'
- 'How could I modify this report to meet more of your requirements?'
- 'What kind of information do you need in order to go forward?'

What sorts of questions are truly worth asking? When we ask questions, we are using a powerful language tool to focus conversational attention and guide our interaction with others. But many of the questions we have learned to ask are totally fruitless and self-defeating (such as, parents to pregnant teenager, 'Why have you done this to us?'). In general it will be more fruitful to ask 'how' questions about the future rather than 'why' questions about the past. Question-asking is one of the main ways that we try to get a grip on whatever is going on, but we are usually not very conscious of the quality of questions we ask. For example:

- 'Why are you always such a fool?'

compared to:

- 'How could we work together to solve this problem?'

Asking questions can allow us to start thinking about the unknown, because questions focus our attention, and provide a theme for continued exploration. There is no straightforward set of rules about how to ask questions that are more helpful or more tuned to the needs of a particular situation. But you can get an intuitive sense of how to do it by studying a wide range of creative questions.

TIP BOX ♀⇨♂

WOMEN COMMUNICATING WITH MEN

- Women should avoid using tag questions (That's an interesting idea, isn't it?') or disclaimers ('I could be mistaken, but -'; 'This may sound strange but -').
- To gain the floor in discussion, women can creatively use strategic questioning. The careful use of questions in a conversation controls when a topic is changed and when a topic is extended and discussed at greater length.
- Women probably should not adopt male behaviour by greatly increasing their rate of interrupting others. Once a woman has the floor, she should resist giving it to another speaker until she has completed her points ('Just a moment, I haven't finished').
- Instead of asking open-ended questions such as, 'How is the project going?' ask closed questions such as 'when can we expect the report of the data structures?'
- Women should not undercut what they are saying with their non-verbal actions. They should adopt a slightly more relaxed posture, do less frequent smiling (and smile only when there is something to smile about), and less frequent nodding, head tilting and dropping of eyes in response to another's gaze. They should avoid using the intonation of a question (raising the voice at the end of a sentence rather than lowering it) when making a declarative statement.

Primary modes

Our perceptions are directly related to the senses – mainly visual, auditory, or kinaesthetic/tactile (sight, sound or movement and touch – but also of course, taste and smell). Although everyone uses all three major styles or modes to interact with the world, most people have a primary one. Research indicates that most people are visually oriented, whereas the fewest number of people are auditorially oriented. To ensure that messages are conveyed, it's important to learn how to communicate in another's particular style. To discover someone's primary mode, you need to:

- listen to the verbs they use
- watch their eye movements during a discussion
- observe their behaviour
- ask how they prefer to receive new information
- be aware of your own preferences.

Here are the three primary modes:

The auditory mode 'I hear what you're saying' or 'It doesn't sound that way to me' are typical statements made by those whose primary way of interacting with the world is auditory. They like to discuss and listen to recorded information and music. When responding to questions or making comments, their eyes will go over to the side, often repeating out loud or in their mind's ear the question or statement made. They will use verbs such as hear, listen, debate, and talk. When presenting new information to them, take the time to discuss it and answer all of their questions.

The kinaesthetic/ tactile mode Many people are doers and are quite demonstrative, preferring movement in their interactions. They often make statements such as 'I feel this is the best solution' or 'I just can't grasp the idea.' When responding to questions or making comments, their eyes will go down to get in touch with emotions and the motion involved in the statement or question. They will use action-oriented verbs such as feel, touch, run, hold, and move. When presenting new information, use hands-on activities, such as actually going through the motions of a new procedure.

The visual mode Visually oriented people interact with the world by creating mental pictures. They make statements such as 'I don't see it that way' or 'It looks good to me.' When responding to questions or making comments, their eyes will go up to create a picture. They also may blink to clear their mind's eye, or they may look directly at you in response to your questions. They will use verbs such as look, see, picture, and imagine. When presenting new information to them, use colourful pictures, charts, or displays.

In these times of doing more with less and increased use of technology, it's imperative to remember to do whatever we can to foster effective communication. Relating to others in a way that makes sense to them will improve relationships, enhance performance, increase productivity, and positively impact the bottom line.

PART 3

MAKING BUSINESS COMMUNICATION WORK

This section looks at different business situations involving communication skills and how men and women can communicate more efficiently with each other and covers:

Setting workplace boundaries
Building rapport and developing trust
Collaboration at work
Giving and receiving feedback
Conducting an interview
Delegating
Meeting skills
Coaching others
Performance management
Negotiation skills
Resolving conflict
Team building
Mentoring others

Setting Workplace Boundaries

Human boundaries are invisible and often violated. Boundaries are limits that are always present, spoken or unspoken, honoured or overstepped. A healthy boundary reflects balance between distance and intimacy, between time spent working and at leisure, between your interests and mine. With healthy interpersonal and personal/professional boundaries you can:

- **work well with those who have bad boundaries**
  For example, the 'human can-opener,' who pries into your personal affairs or the 'time bandit' who doesn't mind stealing your day, 'Really, just 5 minutes' at a time.
- **do your best work, contribute sustainably, ensuring adequate reward for your efforts**
  A healthy personal/professional boundary is the subtle key to maintaining life balance: work at your commitments, do not 'over-perform' or say, 'yes' to unreasonable requests. Get clear on your limits and powerfully express them.
- **get results with literally anyone –** even people you don't happen to like, or with whom you seem to disagree.

How's your skill at honouring other people's boundaries? Do you remember to 'ask permission' before invading their personal space? For example, when initiating a conversation, do you ask, 'Do you have about 10 minutes to go over your comments or should I come back after lunch?' or, 'Are you open to discussing this project right now?' No matter what their response, this says you are aware that you are interrupting, you want their full attention, and are willing to hear their truth.

Whether you're the boss who has too few staff and way too much to do, or you're a member of that staff, establishing and maintaining healthy boundaries is a vital skill set for your sustained success. Setting healthy boundaries – simply stating your truth, from your experience, without fear of retaliation or of hurting the other person's feelings – isn't hard. Ideally, workplace boundary setting takes place in a context of an open discussion about responsibilities, goals and priorities; there's mutual understanding about what needs to be done, and the timeframes are carefully negotiated.

It may seem to men that women overstep boundaries by asking personal questions. To women it may seem that men don't take a holistic perception when relating to them – they may interpret men's boundaries as being impenetrable while they allow their own to be manipulated.

TIP BOX ♀⇆♂

MEN AND WOMEN COMMUNICATING WITH EACH OTHER

Know your limits, know what you want

Knowing your limits is a source of inner strength and helps you focus your energies on what you can do. To protect yourself from going 'overboard,' be organised and on top of your commitments, including knowing yourself and your strengths to give accurate estimates of timeframes. If you regularly put your priorities in writing, it will help you handle unplanned requests or the inevitable reprioritisation in a professional, matter-of-fact way.

Tactfully and openly communicate goals and limits

Sell your abilities by demonstrating what you can get done without selling yourself short by taking on too much. When you talk about your limitations, focus on your positive intention, ask for help in doing your best work, and problem solve, and don't complain about the problem. Pay attention to how the other person is receiving your communication. Be open to feedback; better still, ask for feedback.

... continued overleaf

Be available to discuss differences and get to agreements

Listen and verify your understanding of the other person's needs, interests and concerns. This is a time for using your best communication and win-win negotiation skills. Tune in to their concerns or limits, and look for simple ways to work it out.

Building Rapport and Developing Trust

When we feel pressured or we get uptight, we tend to narrow our peripheral vision, withdraw our senses; we forget that communication is a cooperative system. When communication matters most, where do we put our attention? Our peripheral vision (the ability to hear subtle cues), can help us to avoid psychologically knocking into others. When we put our full attention on the other person (or group), that's an important step in maintaining rapport and flowing with them in collaboration. Before establishing that link, you need to know your goal and what you want out of the interaction. Then you can fully shift your attention to them, and trust that you'll somehow end up where you need to be.

Rapport is the condition of being in sync, in tune, on the same wavelength. In business, rapport is needed to coordinate action and exchange information. Ironically, most business decisions are based on rapport, not on technical merit or the best idea. Rapport makes or breaks most aspects of getting what you want. To maintain an open channel of communication with another person is to align with them, match them, meet them where they are. This doesn't mean you agree with them, necessarily, but rather that you are open and willing to accept their point of view and you let them know you're there with them.

TIP BOX ♀⇆♂

MEN AND WOMEN COMMUNICATING WITH EACH OTHER

Think about a work colleague of the opposite gender. Can you imagine yourself matching his or her basic mood, posture, body language, energy level, tempo and world view? Try this next time you are in a conversation with this person. Pick one or two aspects of behaviour, like voice, tone and tempo, and duplicate it. Say things the way they do. Sit and move as they do. They won't notice that you're being like them - people only notice differences. After you've done that for a while, practice matching their vocabulary, their apparent mood or underlying values, their posture, or their breathing. Are these more of a challenge?

Matching does not have to be direct. Crossover matching (using a different side or other body movement) can be as effective and subtler. By practicing this periodically for several weeks, it becomes even more automatic, and you will fall into step with others more quickly and easily. The purpose of this approach to building rapport (matching and aligning with the other person) is to get fully in step with them, so that the next step you take, they're more likely to follow. When you start by matching and meeting them (not expecting them to come to you), you can take immediate control of the situation and move with greater confidence that they will stay with you.

Developing trust

Trust is probably the single most important ingredient in successful relationships. On the other hand, partly because trust is in our heads – a state of mind, an interpretation, a subjective feeling that develops over time – it is not clear how to reliably improve it. A high degree of trust would permit me to take you on your word, to accept your statements at face value without question. I could give you the 'benefit of the doubt.' We'd be free to derive maximum benefit from our relationship. On the other extreme, a high degree of distrust creates quite a climate of fear, and anxiety would make productive work nearly impossible, shifting the focus from flowing collaboration to suspicious second-guessing, guarded (if any) participation, and probably a pattern of conflict avoidance or passive-aggressiveness. Worse, our moral judgments about each other's untrustworthiness make resolution of these problems quite unlikely.

Most workplace relationships fall somewhere between these two extremes. What's wanted is not just blind trust, but a solid confidence grounded in reality. The challenge: different people give different weight to the importance of being reliable, of keeping a promise.

THE KEY ... is accurately give the degree of trust that is appropriate for that relationship, and necessary for obtaining the results you're after.

In our culture, there is a tendency to think of trust in terms of the other person's trustworthiness. And yet, the one person over whom you have a reasonable amount of control is yourself. Thus, if you focus on whether or not you can trust others, you're just as likely as not, one of these days, to experience distrust. Sooner or later you'll come up with an example of how they 'just can't be trusted.'

A more useful question to ask yourself is, 'Can I predict their behaviour?' Consistency isn't simply a virtue; it is a practical basis for developing effective working relationships. If you can predict someone's behaviour, even if you know they will muck up, you can count on that. This means that the goal is to learn how people operate: pay attention, notice what results they consistently produce and where they get stuck, so you can handle contingencies, mitigate the risks, or involve someone else. For example, when considering delegating a project, ask yourself ,'Will this relationship support these results?' If not, why not? Relationship too new? Results too important to fully delegate and let go? It probably wouldn't work to say, 'I'd like to trust you here, but ...' So what can you do? Talk openly about your concerns, your desire to let them run with it coupled with your conditions of satisfaction.

Trust, like respect, is earned. Think of it as an investment. You observe a person's behaviour over time, and gradually decide whether or not to invest your trust in them. Though everyone initially deserves a base-line of credit, it would be unwise to rely on just anybody in high-risk situations. Women can sometimes be too trusting based on an emotional reaction, whereas men tend to analyse the facts a little more.

Consistency and reliability can be observed and measured; the idea of trust cannot – it's subjective. But people, like the weather, aren't always predictable. And risks will remain – risks of misunderstanding, changed circumstances, and unforeseen events. We must balance focus on the task with building a valued relationship, courage in moving toward our goals with the consideration to involve and include others, healthy scepticism and downside planning with well founded trust.

Trust is somewhere between blind confidence and deep suspicion and fear.

If you want a practical basis for leading your relationships toward greater trust and collaboration, form agreements that bring out people's unique combination of strengths. Having clear goals isn't enough; you want commitment up front to serve as the structure for accountability, feedback, and continuous improvement. As you pinpoint and play to strengths, weaknesses become irrelevant. If a perceived weakness has you questioning a person's trustworthiness, set up an agreement that directly handles your concern. If the person grumbles at your apparent lack of trust, ask, 'How can we work this out so that …?' Agreements serve as a safety net for playing the medium- to high-risk game of business, and with contingency planning, can serve both parties in case things go wrong.

Concerns are low-grade fears. Fear exists for a reason; it intends to protect from harm. Sometimes a fear needs to be surfaced and addressed – unearth the consequence you want to avoid, assess the actual risk vs. potential reward, and do something to mitigate that risk. At other times, it's best to just acknowledge a concern and let it be – such as when there's anxiety, confusion, vague uncertainty or doubt, but not much chance that things will go really wrong. You can ask yourself, 'What's the worst thing that could happen?' and then formulate a plan to safely avoid that consequence.

☞ **If you want others to consider you trustworthy, focus on your own reliability**

How is your own conduct? Are you consistent, and reasonably predictable? Or do you do different things at different times? Some people are so intent on being hard to peg, they'll rearrange their furniture, change their hairstyle, or shift an opinion mid-sentence, just to hear people say, 'How interesting ...' Certainly, some mystery is good and you'll get a better response from people if they understand your motives, intentions and goals.

How do you know if you're seen as trustworthy?
Ask yourself this question:

'To what extent is there alignment between my core values and behaviour, my intentions and actions, my communication and the response I get?'

ANSWER: systematically close the gap.

TIP BOX ♀⇆♂

MEN AND WOMEN COMMUNICATING WITH EACH OTHER

Make fewer and better agreements: This tip isn't suggesting that you intentionally over-commit but rather that you'd damage your credibility if you allowed others to hear a 'yes' when you didn't fully mean it.

Learn to learn: It's more important to be consistent than to be perfect. So when things go pear-shaped, focus on learning how to do it better the next time. Act as if there's no such thing as failure, there's only feedback.

Renegotiate as early as possible: When a promise must be renegotiated, do so early - anticipate - and the focus will be on the agreement and what can be done, not on your reliability, limitations, or whose fault it is.

Renegotiate dysfunctional agreements: If you continually rely on someone that does not produce the goods, you suffer. Over-reliance can be balanced with a good dose of appropriate scepticism and a tighter, renegotiated agreement. A negotiated agreement will help shift the burden of responsibility so that there are two of you trusting.

Say what you mean and mean what you say. Being direct and tactful in equal measures helps others feel safe. If you've got some difficult feedback to deliver, balance your message with positive reinforcement. Say how you feel about it, and encourage them to do the same. As others see you being open and forthcoming, they'll quickly clear up any misunderstandings, be straight and direct, and expect the same. When trust is based on being able to predict the other person's behaviour, you'll have a reason to be curious about how people operate so you can discover and play to their strengths.

Collaboration at Work

Collaboration is necessary and usually advantageous at work in order to gain access to unfamiliar territory and new resources. But collaboration is more than just working together cooperatively (teamwork), more than going along (accommodating) or getting along.

Reflect for a moment on your own workplace. When was the last time you had a conversation that didn't go well? How did you gain resolution? Did you resolve it within yourself ('typical man'), try through a third party ('can you believe what an emotional woman she is') or with the person directly ('I'm sorry, but I don't feel right about X; perhaps there's been a misunderstanding ...'). But this doesn't mean you aren't necessarily collaborating. There are at least four situations where a collaborative approach is essential.

- When you need a more complete perspective, collaboration allows for useful feedback, so rather than hallucinating (filling in blind spots from your own perceptions), you can push back on limited assumptions and gain new awareness.

  SKILLS: distinguishing observation from interpretation, giving feedback and recognition, rapport.

- When there has been a breakdown or problem with another person, collaboration provides the most tactful way of building accountability, trust and safety, while bringing about lasting change.

  SKILLS: Dealing with negativity and blame, establishing accountability, and using the gentle art of confrontation.

- When you need to increase cooperation, collaboration helps deal with differences before they lead to resistance or begin to prevent understanding.

  SKILLS: handling resistance, empathic listening and verifying understanding.

- When you want stewardship (not micro-delegation or micro-management) – whether kicking off an important project or change initiative, stewards 'go slow to go fast' with the right input from all the right players up front.

  SKILLS: asking goal-oriented questions, forming clear and complete agreements, rapport.

TIP BOX ♀⇆♂

MEN AND WOMEN COMMUNICATING WITH EACH OTHER

1 **Courage:** You have the nerve to say what must be said, and you temper it with consideration for the listener so the communication remains two-way. You show integrity when you assert what you know, and by admitting what you don't know. Integrity implies knowing if your communication is based in objective fact, your opinion or a blending of both.

2 **Consideration:** As a sign of respect, you take into account the other person's needs and wants and their present situation without losing focus on the goals at hand. Paradoxically, the more considerate you are, the more tough-minded and courageous you can be without breaking rapport. Considerate also means listening so carefully that you can make requests and offers in ways that fit for the other person.

3 **Consistency:** Are you consistent, not arbitrary or biased, in your business relations? Do you operate out of a set of core values and principles or are you subject to whims? Consistency is the basis for being seen as reliable, dependable, and trustworthy. When you can predict what someone will do, it engenders trust (even if you don't like their behaviour).

4 **Clarity:** You and colleagues are clear about what needs to be done - the goal is explicit and you have acknowledged the complete set of conditions of satisfaction. (cont)

5 Commitment: A solid 'yes' that represents unwavering alignment to give one's best effort. Skilfully check for any unacknowledged resistance or concerns. Surface the downsides to enjoy the upsides.

6 Capacity: This is about one's 'bandwidth,' real-world ability to see it through to completion, to stay focused over time, to clear the path. If one's plate is so full that the new agreement won't fit, the capacity to get the job done is low.

7 Competence: Having the skills and experience to carry out the request properly, and managing your resources so that you can honour all your agreements. This includes renegotiating the minute you notice an agreement that's likely to run aground. Competence also means making request of others to get help, and only making agreements with those who are competent to carry out the request.

Giving and Receiving Feedback

I always like to think of criticism as feedback. You have the same objective but with a different, more user-friendly packaging. Feedback is most useful when it is:

specific	focused on behaviour
positive	useful
supportive	given privately
based on first hand information	fair
given with care	expressed directly
easily acted on	well timed
uncluttered by evaluative judgements	

McGill and Beatty (in 'Action Learning: A Practitioner's Guide', London: Kogan Page, 1994) provide useful suggestions about giving effective feedback:

1. **Clarity:** Be clear about what you want to say.
2. **Emphasise the positive:** This isn't being collusive in the person's dilemma.
3. **Be specific:** Avoid general comments and clarify pronouns such as 'it,' 'that,' etc.
4. **Focus on behaviour** rather than the person.
5. **Refer to behaviour that can be changed.**
6. **Be descriptive** rather than evaluative.
7. **Own the feedback:** Use 'I' statements.
8. **Generalisations:** Notice 'all,' 'never,' 'always,' etc., and ask to get more specificity – often these words are arbitrary limits on behaviour.
9. **Be careful with advice:** People rarely struggle with an issue because of the lack of some specific piece of information; often, the best help is helping the person to come to a better understanding of their issue, how it developed, and how they can identify actions to address the issue more effectively.

Here's are some general pointers when receiving feedback:

- Acknowledge that you heard the person, with a pause, nod, or verbal acknowledgement.
- You can actively prompt feedback of your behaviour, e.g. 'I would like your opinion on how I spoke in that presentation.'
- Honour commonalties more frequently than bringing up the differences. Whatever you refer to most and most intensely will be the centre of your relationship. Keep referring to the part of them and their points that you can support and want to expand upon.
- If the other person does not accept your response at first, consider making the same suggestion later on and in a different way. Do not overlook rearranging the same elements of a suggestion or offer to find a more mutually attractive compromise.
- You can acknowledge that there may be some truth in what is being said, e.g. your response to, 'You never make the coffee' could be, 'I often make the coffee, this week I haven't'.
- Another trick is to note the comment and realise it doesn't belong to you – you can let the speaker know you register their remark but don't respond to it.
- If someone is verbally dumping on you, do not interrupt or counterattack in midstream, or you will only prolong the comments. When the person has finished, ask, 'Is there anything else you want to add?' Then something like, 'What would make this situation better?'
- Ask the individual to propose a solution to the issue raised. If he or she continues to complain or attack, acknowledge you heard the comments each time and, like a broken record, repeat yourself: 'What will make this situation better?' State your view and what you would like from the discussion. Move the other person from a mode of criticising to problem solving. If the other person continues on the downward track of criticism, say, 'I want to find a way to resolve your concern. When do you want to talk about it next?' Then you can remove yourself from the tone of that

discussion and put the other person in the position of initiating follow-up.

- Divide feedback into its parts and respond to the unspoken assumption without playing the victim, e.g. your response to, 'If you had company loyalty, you would do unpaid overtime' could be, 'What do you mean by company loyalty?'
- You can diffuse negative comments with comebacks such as, 'Are you aware of how that remark might sound to other people?'
- If you believe the comments are accurate, then say so. Then say what you plan to do differently to respond to the feedback. Ask for a response to your comments.
- If you disagree with the comments, say, 'May I tell you my perspective?' This sets the other person up to give you permission to state your view, as you have been willing to listen to his or hers.
- You can agree with the true feedback of negative qualities, e.g. your response to, 'You haven't telephoned me lately' could be, 'I agree I haven't called you in the last two weeks'.
- Ask the person to clarify or expand any statement.
- Especially in the beginning, listen more and talk less, keep your motions and voice lower and slower. These behaviours increase the chances that others will feel more safe and comfortable around you.

And some general pointers on giving feedback:

- Be specific, e.g. 'Red doesn't suit your colouring' as opposed to 'You've got no idea of what colours suit you' or mention the specifics of the action done that you want to provide feedback on.
- Acknowledge the positive.
- Give feedback within a situation that you can both relate to.
- Focus on behaviour rather than the person and refer to behaviour that can be changed.
- Ask for what you want the other person to do differently in the future.

- Keep calm.
- Avoid labels such as 'typical woman or typical man'.
- Explain why you want what you're asking for or the reason you think the other person should change, e.g. 'When you do A (observation), I feel B (emotion): I want you to do C (requested change) because of D (purpose).'
- Be descriptive rather than evaluative or judgmental.
- Let the feedback be well timed – as near the event as possible.

Women often feel uncomfortable about giving feedback – they don't want to be responsible for hurting another person's feelings (they need to realise they aren't responsible for the reactions of others – we are only responsible for ourselves). When receiving feedback, women can become upset because they often take it as an indictment on their personality as opposed to an observation on their behaviour. Men can sometimes experience feedback from women as being an attack on their capability. I like the 'sandwich technique' when giving feedback. Say something positive, lay out the constructive feedback and finish with something positive.

TIP BOX ♀⇨♂

WOMEN COMMUNICATING WITH MEN

- Avoid blaming or bad labelling language such as, 'You don't know what you are talking about.'
- Keep to the point and don't bring in irrelevances.

TIP BOX ♂⇨♀

MEN COMMUNICATING WITH WOMEN

- Empathise with the other person's situation or feelings.
- Take into account the needs of both the receiver and giver.
- Clarify your feelings about the action and take responsibility for your part in the interaction and avoid laying blame on the other.

Conducting an Interview

Interviews are particularly useful for getting the story behind a participant's experiences and to pursue in-depth information around a topic. Before you start to design your interview questions and process, clearly identify what need is to be addressed, using the information to be gathered by the interviews. This helps you keep clear focus on the intent of each question.

Types of interviews:

Informal, conversational interview	No predetermined questions are asked.
General interview	This approach is intended to ensure that the same general areas of information are collected from each interviewee.
Standardised, open-ended interview	Here, the same open-ended questions are asked to all interviewees. This approach facilitates faster interviews that can be more easily analysed and compared.
Closed, fixed-response interview	Where all interviewees are asked the same questions and asked to choose answers from among the same set of alternatives.

Here's are some general pointers to bearing in mind when conducting an interview:

- Observe contact reaction as the subject walks into your office or the interviewing space. Remember that seventy percent of all communication is non-verbal.
- Develop a set of questions and ask the same questions of each candidate. If you want to distinguish one person from another,

you have to get a range of responses. The way to do this is to ask the exact same questions of each candidate, and then compare their answers.

- Start with stereotypical interview questions, but be aware that your purpose in doing so is to make the subject comfortable. Then take off from there and go deeper. Your objective is to get the subject talking, in as much of a discursive, narrative fashion as possible.
- Sample all relevant areas of the candidate's life such as: work, education, health, social life, childhood, family and personality. In each category, however, start the candidate talking about something he knows like the back of his hand. Go from the impersonal to the personal. Go from the familiar to the unfamiliar. Go from the intellect to the emotions.
- Take notes or tape record the interview (with permission).
- Maintain a steady presence from one interview to the next. Do not behave one way toward one candidate, and an entirely different way toward another. To unduly influence one candidate toward a negative, or defensive, reaction and another candidate toward a positive reaction is, again, to compromise your interview data.
- Consider the interview as a real-life or on-the-job process. In effect, the ideal way to look upon an interview is as a laboratory to sample projected workplace behaviour by the candidates. Within the bounds of necessary time limits, you as the interviewer should set up interactions and experiments that will represent possible scenarios on the job.
- Do not err on the side of being afraid of asking penetrating questions. Be professional, be courteous, and demonstrate a genuine interest in the person you are interviewing. This is the way to build trust, and trust is critical to success in gaining insight into each candidate.
- Be aware that the toughest challenge in the interview process is interpreting the data. Many interviewers see the discussion process as the most important aspect of interviewing. In reality,

the true meaning of the interview will only emerge with skilful interpretation of the data you have gathered. Proper interpretation of data involves matching a given candidate with a given job in such a way that the organisation is assured that the tasks assigned to that job will be carried out well, and that the person will mesh well with others in the organisation's culture.

- Before asking about controversial matters (such as feelings and opinions), first ask about some facts. With this approach, respondents can more easily engage in the interview before warming up to more personal matters.
- Intersperse opinion-based questions throughout the interview to avoid long lists of fact-based questions, which tends to leave respondents disengaged.
- Ask questions about the present before questions about the past or future. It's usually easier for them to talk about the present and then work into the past or future.
- Wording of questions should be open-ended. Respondents should be able to choose their own terms when answering questions.
- Questions should be as neutral as possible. Avoid wording that might influence answers, e.g. evocative wording. Questions should be worded clearly. This includes knowing any terms particular to the programme or the respondent's culture.
- Be careful when asking 'why' questions. This type of question infers a cause-effect relationship that may not truly exist. These questions may also cause respondents to feel defensive, e.g. that they have to justify their response, which may inhibit their responses to this and future questions.
- Note and address terms of confidentiality. Explain who will get access to their answers and how their answers will be analysed.
- Explain the format of the interview. Explain the type of interview you are conducting and its nature. If you want them to ask questions, specify if they're to do so as they have them or wait until the end of the interview.

- Don't count on your memory to recall their answers. Ask for permission to record the interview or bring along someone to take notes.
- Encourage responses with occasional nods of the head, 'uh huh's, etc.
- Provide transition between major topics, e.g. 'We've been talking about ... and now I'd like to move on to ...'
- Don't lose control of the interview. This can occur when respondents stray to another topic, take so long to answer a question that times begins to run out, or even begin asking questions to the interviewer.
- Write down any observations made during the interview. For example, where did the interview occur and when, was the respondent particularly nervous at any time? Were there any surprises during the interview?

TIP BOX ♀⇨♂

WOMEN COMMUNICATING WITH MEN

- Do not hasten to put the candidate at ease. The mental and emotional state of candidates as they enter into the interviewing process is important data. It can tell you a lot about how they relate to new people and what their self-concept is. If nervousness persists on the part of the candidate, then you can use some techniques to put the person at ease.
- Attempt to remain as neutral as possible. That is, don't show strong emotional reactions to their responses.

TIP BOX ♂⇨♀

MEN COMMUNICATING WITH WOMEN

- Note the emotional flavour of the interview. Keeping yourself steady as a measuring instrument, you will observe that different candidates will bring to the interview into a type of emotional atmosphere. Some interviews will feel warm and open to you; others may feel cold and closed. This should be an indication of the kind of atmosphere a subject will help to generate in the workplace.

Delegating

How do you delegate? Here are eight key steps to successful delegation:

1 First decide which tasks to delegate

- Identify tasks with sensitive implications and keep them.
- Identify tasks, which others may enjoy more than yourself and give them to others.
- Identify task with global or cross-unit impacts and keep them.
- Identify tasks which others may be more skilful at completing and give them to others.

2 Then plan the delegation

- Further review details of each task.
- Establish performance standards.
- Clarify appropriate limits of authority.
- Provide a training support or a back-up person.

3 Select a member of the team

- Match task to interests and skills.
- Balance challenge with support.
- Consider member developmental needs.
- Be sure not to overload the member.

4 Communicate responsibilities to team members

- Set SMART goals (Specific, Measurable, Attainable, Relevant, Trackable).
- Develop clear understanding of goals with team member.
- Define relative importance of the goals and task to the team member.
- Explain the potential complications.
- Stay results oriented, not procedure oriented.

- Set performance standards for the task.
- Communicate consequences of superior, good and bad performance.

5 Assign the task

- Clarify degree of authority.
- Identify constraints.
- Spell out specifics of the task.
- Identify priorities within the task.
- State deadlines for completion.

6 Provide the appropriate level of support

- Let team members know what available resources are.
- Give notice to others that the team member will be working with the team member's new responsibilities.
- Communicate how much you will be available to help.

7 Follow up

- Initiate contact for further direction/support.
- Encourage different styles of task management.
- Continue communication opportunities during the process.
- Allow for mistakes.
- Insist on updates from members.
- Record performance and offer appropriate feedback.

8 Evaluate the delegation

- Compare results of the task with the initial goals; why was or wasn't the delegation successful?
- Evaluate team member's role during the delegation. Did he or she handle the level of authority granted? Could the person handle more authority next time? Evaluate team member on efficiency, timing, creativity, co-operation.
- Discuss your evaluation with team members.
- Provide team member with constructive criticism, both positive and negative feedback.

When you delegate, you distribute responsibility and authority to others while holding them accountable for their performance. The ultimate accountability, however, still lies with you. That's why you must establish appropriate controls and checkpoints to monitor progress. Your role is to set clear goals and expectations for the assignment without telling the worker how to do it. This way, you allow others to discover for themselves the best way to follow through.

Here are some general steps in becoming a master at delegation:

Avoid perfection	Instead of striving for perfection, establish a standard of quality and provide a time frame for reaching it. Then let your team choose any reasonable means to reach that goal.
Give effective instruction	Make sure your worker has enough information to complete the job successfully.
Support your workers	Communicate your expectations before work begins, then tell your team what you expect from them and what support they can expect from you.
Follow-up on progress	After you delegate a task to a worker, leave them to do the work, but check on their progress.
Praise the efforts of your team	A few words of praise, a brief note or a handshake goes a long way in expressing to your workers how much you appreciate their skills and talents.
Recognise that others have ability	Sometimes managers believe that only they can do something the right way. This belief often develops because a worker handles an assignment differently than a supervisor would.
Know your true interests	Delegation is difficult for some people who actually prefer doing the work themselves rather than managing it. Ironically, people are often promoted to management as a result of their technical excellence rather than their ability to manage.
Trust your team	If you do not trust members of your team, take time to consider why. Ask yourself if your own

actions may be the root cause for your lack of trust e.g. have you delegated authority as well as responsibility?

Delegation isn't all or nothing

Because of your team's varying skills and confidence levels, tasks often need to be delegated gradually. As a worker becomes more competent and confident, you can give him or her more authority and accountability.

Delegation as teaching

Workers are reluctant to accept a delegated responsibility when mistakes are more frequently punished than accepted as part of learning. Your willingness to accept mistakes will encourage your team to accept assignments.

TIP BOX ♂⇨♀

MEN COMMUNICATING WITH WOMEN

- Maintain enough personal security in your own position so you don't feel threatened by delegation.

TIP BOX ♀⇨♂

WOMEN COMMUNICATING WITH MEN

- Become willing to take risks.

Empowerment is a little like delegation – responsibility and power that managers grant workers. The reality today is that many front line workers already have a lot of power. The key is to recognise their power and motivate them to channel it in the interests of the business.

- Workers who serve customers and knowledge workers (those who require specialist knowledge to complete their work) whose innovations are crucial, have the power to make or break your business. You cannot empower them, you just need to acknowledge how important and powerful they already are.

- Workers are doing the most critical jobs and managers are increasingly seen as facilitators or coaches who simply need to get out of the way and let the powerful workers do the business. Nevertheless, it is hard for workers to fully utilise their power because the other reality is that managers still have the power to promote or fire them, so both sides have their own sort of power and today the balance is more even than it used to be.
- An even balance of power implies partnership, not empowerment – the catch is that partners expect an even balance of reward distribution as well. The key here is not so much to empower workers who are already powerful but to motivate them to channel their power to maximise business results.

TIP BOX ♀⇆♂

MEN AND WOMEN COMMUNICATING WITH EACH OTHER

How to empower people:

- First your culture has to adjust, then people have to be developed to overcome their fear of acting without your approval
- Many workers are already more than able to take all the responsibility you can give them
- Get people to realise how much power they have already - through their specialist skills and knowledge
- The hardest part of empowerment is changing old habits - your willingness to let go and fearful workers to abandon their fears
- Trust takes time to build - regular feedback- both to the manager and to the empowered worker will build their confidence

Empower when:

- workers are close to customers
- innovation is critical
- the individuals concerned are ready
- close supervision is impossible
- the boss can genuinely let go
- the boss is supportive and a good coach
- technology is complex
- processes are changing rapidly
- the environment is uncertain
- workers demand growth, responsibility and development
- initiative has a high payoff value
- workers need motivating.

Consider not empowering when:

- consistency and uniformity across workers and time are essential
- costs need to be minimised and tightly controlled
- the organisation's culture is not supportive
- the managers are not ready to let go
- operations need to be standardised
- errors are too costly
- workers are untrained or otherwise not ready
- workers are too dependent and lack confidence
- individual initiative may be too costly
- motivation is already strong the way things are
- close supervision is essential

Empowerment may fail for any one of several reasons:

- the feeling that, 'Only I can make the right decisions'
- fear of having nothing to do – being redundant or having no purpose
- fear of losing face or status
- not accepting that subordinates are more knowledgeable or better placed to make some decisions
- lack of support from the organisation's culture – demands for

more centralised decision-making
- preaching the value of making mistakes while still punishing them
- the manager's fear of losing power
- pressure from the manager's boss to be on top of all details
- rationalisation that workers are not ready
- fear of losing control.

TIP BOX ♀⇆♂

MEN AND WOMEN COMMUNICATING WITH EACH OTHER

A 3-stage skills model of empowering others:

- **Exploration**

  A enables B to explore problem from B's perspective and to focus on specific concerns.

- **Understanding**

  B is helped to see themselves in a new perspective and to focus on what they might do to cope more effectively. They are helped to see what strengths and resources they might use.

- **Action**

  B is helped to consider possible ways to act, to look at consequences, to plan action, implement it and evaluate.

Meeting Skills

Any meeting gives you a great opportunity to increase your visibility as a powerful and knowledgeable communicator. There are several reasons to have a meeting:

- to develop networks
- to exchange ideas and experience
- to review whether a decision in action is working
- to decide upon a proposal
- to discuss a decision made elsewhere
- development of teamwork
- to support
- to share information
- to get members views and proposals
- to discuss what the group needs to be doing
- to carry out legal business
- to learn.

Types of meeting:

Informative/advisory	to give and receive information to keep in touch to co-ordinate activities to record progress towards goals
Decision taking	to generate commitment to take decisions to share responsibilities to initiate action
Negotiating	to create an agreement to find a solution
Consultative	to resolve objections to involve people

	to get to know people
Problem solving	to create ideas to identify alternative action to initiate action

When you have found what the objectives of the meeting are, prepare to be supportive and encouraging. Aim to earn authority as a leader among equals. Be resourceful and collaborate on objectives. Participate and become involved. Good participation means:

- learning about issues
- listening to others
- thinking before you speak
- speaking clearly and to the point
- being reasonable
- having confidence in yourself.

To gain recognition, sit within good eye contact of decision-makers. If presenting, arrive early and select your vantage point. If it is a long table, choose the middle of one side, if it is an oval table, choose one of the narrow curved ends. To mitigate a confrontation, sit next to the challenger. To avoid attention, sit in a blind spot for the Chair, wear a neutral outfit with no accessories.

Good communication isn't only about what you say but also about your non-verbal signals. Undermining signals include:

- slouching in your chair
- looking down at your notes out of the window
- looking up at the ceiling
- turning away
- folding arms across the body
- using closed, threatening gestures
- a deadpan or cynical expression.

Positive signals include:

- sitting upright and alert
- sitting forward
- keeping your eyes on the speaker
- taking notes on key points
- turning body to speaker

- opening your body language
- smiling

Key words to use in meetings

save	safety	evaluate	proven
discover	guarantee	results	you
update	complete	endorsed	maximise
image	value	inform	sure
quality	personal	affect	best
venture	customer	future	empower
practical	skills	facilitate	able
advantage	brilliant	confidence	controlled
detail	economical	effective	emphasis
now	outstanding	professional	volume
tremendous	top	today	money-making
lowest cost	latest	key	instant
impelling	immediate	help	quality
quickly	results	satisfaction	smart
solved	special	successful	expert
excited	fair	new	knowledge
valid	reliable	original	fast
reliable	measure	motivate	involve

17 factors for successful participation:

1. If attending a meeting for the first time, introduce yourself.
2. Make an impression by preparing ideas for agenda items that interest you.
3. Speak up at least once during every meeting you attend.
4. Familiarise yourself with the group dynamics of any new meeting you attend.
5. Study the agenda prior to the meeting.
6. Arrive early so that you can get to know others.
7. Know who's who.
8. Use powerful body language and verbal language.
9. Speak slowly and clearly and with authority.
10. Take credit for your ideas.

11 If you are aware that conflict may arise, plan for it and prepare to compromise.
12 Don't allow an argument turn into a free-for-all.
13 Sit where you can be seen and heard (near to the head or to the right of someone with power).
14 If you anticipate conflict sit on that person's dominate (are they left or right-handed?) side so that they will feel less threatened.
15 If you want to exert an influence speak early in a discussion.
16 Maintain eye contact.
17 Use your hands to express your point.

Chairing a meeting

The agenda should contain:

- organisation name
- committee/group name
- date, time and place of meeting, and finishing time
- apologies
- welcome
- minutes of last meeting
- matters arising
- specifics
- any other business
- future meeting details.

Minutes are used to record what is being decided, why it was decided, what action is to be taken, when and by whom and what else was discussed. Minutes should include:

1 organisational name
2 date, time and place
3 meeting description
4 people present
5 apologies for absence
6 who chaired
7 corrections to previous minutes
8 matters arising from previous meeting
9 minutes for topics for this meetings (specific reference needs to be made to any decisions taken and action to be taken, by

whom and when by) – it is a good idea to number minutes sequentially through a series of meetings to facilitate references and changes
10 date, time and place of next meeting
11 time this meeting finished.

When dealing with difficult people in a meeting, you need to be able to deal with those who want to argue, who won't listen, the person who talks too much or the person who makes fixed statements. At times like this, you need to move the issue away from them and back into the wider group. You could do this by restating the issue or it may be that the best way of moving the meeting forward is by allowing controlled discussion. Other techniques you could use include: intervention, asking for clarification, acknowledging high feelings, summarising and then moving the topic on, injecting a little humour, asking direct questions and using people's names.

As the person in the chair, you could see an extension to your role as that of facilitator. This is where you enable individuals in a meeting to interact with each other, even to the extent of using conflict as a tool for discovery and growth. A facilitator will create an atmosphere of support and openness and will encourage group members to express their feelings and contribute their ideas.

Some general pointers for successful Chairing:

- The Chair needs to impose a firm discipline on proceedings.
- When setting the agenda, consider your objectives and enclose any papers relevant to the meeting. Send at least a week in advance.
- Meetings held in the morning are more productive.
- Assign someone to take minutes.
- Open the meeting on a positive note.
- Introduce each agenda subject via a brief overview.
- Keep the meeting moving by keeping focused on the current agenda subject. Keep your pre-set timescales for each area in mind.
- Summarise occasionally and call for a decision when appropriate.
- Encourage controlled discussion.

- Finish the meeting with a summary of main points, action to be taken and by whom as well as any decisions taken
- Follow up the action to be taken via smaller meetings or individual sessions.
- People attending a meeting should be encouraged to participate.
- Successful meetings depend upon a strong chairperson.

The Chair's attitude to the meeting will be reflected in the attitudes of the group members to each other during the meeting.

TIP BOX ♀⇨♂

WOMEN COMMUNICATING WITH MEN

- Organise supporting materials, anticipate problems and be ready with solutions.
- Remain impartial when emotions run high. Separate facts from opinion and clarify points.
- Focus the meeting on problem solving.
- It may sometimes be necessary to ignore the feelings of others in order to reach a group decision.
- At decision-making meetings, place the emphasis on whether the decision is the right one as opposed to whether members are happy with the outcome.

TIP BOX ♂⇨♀

MEN COMMUNICATING WITH WOMEN

- Chairing a meeting is more about listening than talking.
- Make people feel positive and important. Acknowledge their contributions and use their names when you do so.

Coaching Others

FOUR principles of coaching:

- **Providing support to others**
- **Listening and responding with empathy**
- **Sharing thoughts and feelings and rationale**
- **Maintaining coachee's self-esteem**

Coaching is a form of leading – you lead people to think differently. Coaching means asking questions, which lead others to new insights, and helping people solve their own problems. One of the challenges in coaching is to resist always offering your answers, otherwise you are feeding them fish rather than teaching them to fish for themselves. Also, people commit themselves most fully to their own solutions.

Coaching helps people do any occupational task more effectively and has the objective of helping high performers reach greater heights.

Advice can be helpful but only short term – not to replace helping others to think for themselves. This means asking open ended, non-judgemental questions to stimulate broader thinking on their part. When the people receiving coaching get off track, ask them to consider certain implications of their preferred course of action rather than telling them your answers. As a last resort, when you need to give someone the answer, pose it as a question: 'How do you think this approach would work for you?' Avoid closing down too quickly on a solution – strive to dig deeper into how the other person thinks by probing with further open questions, such as: 'I wonder what leads you to that view?' or 'Can you help me understand your reasoning there?' Acknowledge any insights gained and good points made. Ask what they will do differently and by when. Strive always in coaching to maintain and enhance the other person's self esteem.

Your team can grow much faster if you assume a coaching role. Team members need training and support to help them gain their full power to perform the team's work as well as to perform work as a team. If you are going to help your team develop needed skills, you must cultivate a set of coaching skills including listening, communicating, advocating, team building, facilitating decision-making, training, educating, and mentoring.

Hierarchical 'command and control' management practices are giving way to more collaborative, fluid and dynamic structures. Why? People naturally perform better when their work environment matches how they like being treated. The challenge of letting go of control and authoritative practices is that few people know how to manage the transition. There's fear and scepticism around change anyway, so this just adds to the confusion. The management task is to let go of control in favour of new structures and accountability agreements. To assist people in using structures and forming clear and complete agreements, many organisations are using cross-functional teams and providing training in coaching skills.

TIP BOX ♀⇆♂

MEN AND WOMEN COMMUNICATING WITH EACH OTHER

Be present: The more you can be present, the better you will be as a coach. Being present means being on their agenda, available to what they're up to, able to let them know you understand their situation, challenges, resistance, fears, etc. Like rapport, this element is foundational to all others.

Clear goals: Set clear immediate goals and long-term direction with 'What do you want?' and 'How will you know when you've got that?'

... continued overleaf

Ask vs. tell: Giving unsolicited advice is not only disempowering, it's unnecessary. Resist the temptation to 'give them a fish;' instead, teach them how to fish for their own answers. If you feel compelled to offer advice, it can be packaged in a way that puts the person fully at choice and in charge.

Agreements: Unclear or incomplete agreements produce misery and suffering. This also includes effective agreements for how they want to be coached. Clear agreements can contribute to setting an atmosphere of mutual respect and shared power. Effective coaching turns up the volume on accountability to agreements, replacing the need for 'command and control.'

Recognition: Don't make the mistake of giving fake praise or no praise. Instead look for what it is about this person and their performance that's praise-worthy and be sincere in your encouragement.

Feedback: Let their mistakes be their best teacher. Live by 'no failure; only feedback' and only give constructive suggestions for improvement. Separate the person from the issue. Provide both observation and interpretation so you can openly discuss differing perceptions.

Structure: Design reasonable action steps to reach achievable goals. Structures are for supporting, not burdening, the client. They assist the client to systematically assess and adjust priorities, to increase their capacity to focus, and to track progress for on-going learning and process improvement.

Intuiting: The opposite of structure. Intuition is different from opinion or interpretation. Intuition usually comes from a 'gut feel' or other body signals. An effective coach knows when to throw away the plan, be pragmatic, and how to politely invade or challenge the client's assumptions to prevent catastrophe.

Performance Management

Performance management reminds us that training, strong commitment and lots of hard work alone are not results. The major contribution of performance management is its focus on achieving results. Performance management redirects our efforts away from busy-ness toward effectiveness.

Increasing competition from across the world has meant that businesses must be more careful about the choice of strategies to remain competitive. This situation has put more focus on effectiveness and means that systems and processes in the organisation must be applied in the right way to the right things in order to achieve results. All of the results across the organisation must continue to be aligned to achieve the overall results desired by the organisation for it to survive and thrive. Then the organisation and its various parts are really performing.

Typically when we think of performance in organisations, we think on the performance of employees. However, performance management should also be focused on:

- the organisation
- projects, e.g. automating the billing process
- teams or groups organised to accomplish a result for internal or external customers
- departments, e.g. computer support
- processes, e.g. billing
- programs, e.g. implementing new policies and procedures to ensure a safe workplace
- products or services to internal or external customers.

Feedback is information relevant to how well results are being achieved. Useful feedback is timely, feasible and understood. Ideally, feedback address key activities to improve or reinforce performance. Usually, the larger the number of sources giving feedback, the more accurate is the depiction of events. Any ideas to improve or support performance should be implemented as appropriate.

A performance appraisal (or review) includes documentation of expected results, standards of performance, progress toward achieving of results, how well they were achieved, examples indicating achievement, suggestions to improve performance and how those suggestions can be followed. The performance appraisal should be carried out at regular intervals as performance tracking is under way. From here, there are two routes.

1 If performance meets desired performance standards, reward for performance.

2 If performance does not meet standards, implement a performance development plan. This plan clearly conveys how the conclusion was made that there was inadequate performance, what actions are to be taken and by whom and when, when performance will be reviewed again and how. Inadequate performance does not always indicate a problem on the part of the worker. Performance standards may be unrealistic or the worker may have insufficient resources. Similarly, the overall strategies or the organisation may be unrealistic or without sufficient resources. When performance management is applied to an employee or group of employees, a development plan can be initiated in a variety of situations such as:

- when a performance appraisal indicates performance improvement is needed
- as part of succession planning to help an employee be eligible for a planned change in role in the organisation
- to pilot the operation of a new performance management system
- to benchmark the status of improvement so far in a development effort
- as part of a professional development for the employee or group of employees

TIP BOX ♀⇆♂

MEN AND WOMEN COMMUNICATING WITH EACH OTHER

1 Know the attitudes and personality traits of the individual you are confronting.

2 Be sure your own attitude is one of genuine helpfulness. If you are criticising only to show your authority, you will not be successful. Never confront in anger. Always allow yourself time to calm down and think coolly before approaching someone regarding improvement of performance.

3 Get all the facts first. If possible, find the cause of the behaviour or error before you talk with the person. Do not embarrass yourself by reprimanding an employee before making sure of the facts. Errors are often due to factors beyond the control of the employee. In getting the facts, don't make snap judgements. Give the employee a fair hearing. Let the employee tell his or her side of the story fully. Be a good listener as attention to the story may bring out important points that you might otherwise overlook.

4 Share the responsibility for an error. A good supervisor/manager tries to let the employee save face. Your job is to correct and improve behaviour and performance – not embarrass the employee.

5 Don't belittle the employee. Personal abuse wounds the ego to the extent it's not possible to listen to your suggestions with an open mind. Such criticism is likely to frustrate! On the other hand, constructive suggestions will motivate an employee to improve.

6 Be tactful without emotion. Have patience. Never use sarcasm or ridicule.

7 People respond much better if they believe that their supervisor/manager has faith in them and thinks they have the ability and intelligence to do the job correctly. Don't seek to establish blame. Seek the cause of the error or action with the employee. Make the cause clear. Show the way to eliminate it and how to substitute the right action. Explain how and why the work must be done in the manner expected.

Negotiation Skills

The basics of effective negotiation are:

- ☑ clear communication
- ☑ give and take
- ☑ decision making skills
- ☑ keeping focused
- ☑ empathy
- ☑ persuasive communication
- ☑ understanding other people's needs
- ☑ anticipating responses
- ☑ projecting yourself

All too often negotiation is seen as a 'I win' situation but true negotiation needs to be a 'I win – You win' situation. Win-win negotiations need to:

- be on seeking common ground
- be related to the other party and they concerns
- be ready to compromise
- yield the highest level of commitment from others
- be based on mutual respect and trust
- involve harder work than using force or manipulation
- full and equal involvement
- facilitate two-way discussions
- involve questioning and listening techniques
- involve the disclosure of appropriate information
- aim for agreement not stalemate
- seek mutual gains.

Variables are the raw material used in preparing for negotiation:

- consider the other people involved and their needs and possible objections, find out their intentions
- consider your own position
- set realistic objectives
- structure the meeting
- decide how variables can be used to trade

Tips for conducting the negotiation:

Opening

- Recap contacts, agreements so far
- You could take the hard approach (indicating little will be given away)
- You could take the soft approach (best for unclear situations)

Main body

- Use specific variables and keep looking for additional variables
- Use a promise of reward
- Use a threat of punishment, e.g. not giving something
- Use hooks, e.g. 'My chairman says ... '
- Build a bridge of rapport through:
  - discussing neutral subjects
  - obtaining initial agreement
  - presenting options for the other person in your offering
  - referring back to past agreement to reinforce persuasion
  - stating clear objectives.
- Show confidence
- Get the other parties' position firmly in your mind
- Start trading early.
  - Be seen to drive a hard bargain
  - Optimise your concessions
  - Minimise their concessions
  - Play down your gratitude for concessions gained
  - Build up the value of concessions you make
  - If you can't optimise or minimise, stay silent
- Put your major issue cards on the table
- Summarise frequently
- Avoid confrontation and maintain neutrality
- Treat disagreements carefully
- Bide your time and don't push too hard
- Make notes
- Leave people feeling each move forward is a

positive one for them

- Read between the lines
- Don't act precipitately
- Remain professional
- Resolve to lead albeit in a subtle way
- Use verbal and non-verbal language to your advantage
- Keep your concentration focused and adopt a calm and considered approach
- Don't underestimate the other party
- Don't exaggerate facts
- Don't overreact if responses are negative
- Don't let yourself be affected by psychological warfare e.g. pretended misunderstanding
- Don't put the other party on their guard, provide time for them to react well
- Avoid deadlock – always search for variables
- Don't agree to something you don't want
- Aim to end on a pleasant note

Agreement

- Is a formal or informal contract required?
- Set the policy and content of any contractual arrangements

The best in influencing skills involve:

- inviting an opinion from someone who as not been given an opportunity to contribute
- restoring a sense of proportion and relieving tension
- reminding people of the stage they've reached.

TIP BOX ♀⇨♂

WOMEN COMMUNICATING WITH MEN

- Don't allow yourself to become over-emotional.

TIP BOX ♂⇨♀

MEN COMMUNICATING WITH WOMEN

- Acknowledge and reconcile others' views.
- Ask questions and listen to the answers.
- Build relationships.

Resolving Conflict

Showing negativity

Being able to respond positively to negativity in others is a crucial part of relationship skills. By understanding some of the ways that negative behaviour comes out in others (and that we might show to others), we can change a potentially damaging situation into something much more positive. Some of the ways we can show our negativity to others, and they to us, include:

Blaming

Example:	'It's all your fault.'
Alternative:	'From my perspective, it seems as if both you and Tony may have contributed to what's happened. Maybe we can all have a chat about it.'

Over-interpreting

Example:	'I think you're afraid of having authority and that's why you're not going for that job.'
Alternative:	'Tell me more about your fears over the new job.'

Not accepting another's feelings

Example:	'Don't get depressed about it.'
Alternative:	'I can understand why you feel depressed.'

Faking attention

Example:	'That is interesting.'
Alternative:	Don't fake it, mean it – or don't say anything at all.

Placing time pressures

Example: 'Make it quick, I've got a meeting in five minutes.'

Alternative: 'I haven't much time right now as I'm off to a meeting. Could we meet later to talk about this?'

Directing

Example: 'I would like you to talk about your relationship with your line manager.'

Alternative: 'Is there anything bothering you at the moment?'

Labelling

Example: 'You just being neurotic.'

Alternative: 'Why do you think you feel like that?'

Unwanted advice

Example: 'If I were you ... '

Alternative: 'Would you like to talk about this? Maybe I can help.'

Putting on the spot

Example: 'Are you busy on Thursday afternoon?'

Alternative: 'I need some extra help on Thursday afternoon. Are you free at all?'

Nagging

Example: 'Haven't you done the work I gave you yet?'

Alternative: 'When will you complete the work?'

Preaching

Example: 'Promotion isn't everything in life.'

Alternative: 'How do you feel about not getting the promotion?'

Lecturing

Example: 'We should co-operate and then there would be less tension.'

Alternative: 'What can we do to solve this problem?'

Aggression

Example: 'Fool!'

Alternative: 'I'm angry with what you've done/said. Can we talk?'

Judging

Example: 'You're not very good at expressing yourself.'
Alternative: 'How might you be able to improve relations between you and Joan?'

Interrogating

Example: 'Tell me about your weaknesses.'
Alternative: 'How do you see yourself?'

More negotiations break down over ego differences than over content differences. Ironically, the person who has the most to teach you right now is the person you perceive to be the biggest twit in your life. Understanding how you can have more positively powerful reactions to their difficult behaviour will give you more options around that person and others who also prove difficult.

TIP BOX

MEN AND WOMEN COMMUNICATING WITH EACH OTHER

What causes people to like you and agree with you? The two main predictors of someone's behaviour toward you are:

- their 'operating manual', which they are constantly showing you by their strongest reactions to others
- the manner in which they characterise the good and bad behaviours of others.

You also need to learn where people put their most intense energy and attention:

- their hot buttons or blind spots, e.g. what makes them angry or afraid
- their points of pride, e.g. what makes them happy or confident.

You will find it more difficult to recognise others' blind spots and points of pride in people for whom you already have strong negative or positive feelings. It is easier to determine the areas in people you know less well or feel less strongly about. You can build a connection with someone when you either:

1. help them through times that bring up their 'hot buttons' … or
2. align with one of the parts of themselves they most like.

Building good relationships

Here are some tips to building genuine good will and enduring relationships:

Make them shine

If people don't like the way they are when they are around you, they will blame you for it – and not be aware they are doing so. They will sabotage projects on which you're working even to their own detriment. They will fail to give you credit and see qualities in you they don't like in other people. On the other hand, if people like the way they are when they are around you, they will see in you the qualities they like in other people (even if you don't demonstrate you have them), give you generous credit, and go out of their way to help you.

Give up front

To show your commitment to reaching agreement, offer something up front, unasked.

Demonstrate consistent, visible good will

As a daily habit to all, not just to important contacts, remember people form first impressions in the first seven to twenty seconds, which take a significant emotional event to change.

Sidle

People are more likely to like each other, remember more of what they discuss, and agree when they 'sidle,' standing or sitting side by side, rather than facing each other. Two women or a man and a woman are more likely to face each other. Two men instinctively sidle. Sidling creates rapport between people. Walking and talking gets you further connected. The best time to resolve issues is while walking together to the meeting, not when you are in the meeting, sitting across from each other.

Look for the underlying issue

When you are arguing for more than ten minutes, you are probably not discussing the real conflict and are thus unlikely to get it resolved in the discussion. Look for the underlying issue.

Detect lying earlier

When lying, most people can put an innocent expression on their face when you ask them a question about the topic, yet few get the right timing or duration of that expression. Ignore the expression itself when they respond but note whether they appear to put it on too soon or too late and if the duration of the expression seems off. Here your instincts will often guide you to knowing their truthfulness.

The more opportunities you provide for others to participate in a situation along the way, the more likely they will stay with you to ultimately find a solution.

Be vividly specific

A vivid, specific detail is memorable, while a general statement is less credible and easily forgotten. Ironically, most adult conversation and advertising is general. Children are more likely to be vividly specific and thus more memorable. When you want to be heard and remembered, characterise your information or request with a vivid, specific detail, example, story or contrasting options. Involve words that relate to the senses. For example ‘beautiful colour’ is not as vivid as ‘blue’ which is not as vivid as ‘cobalt blue.’

Be ‘plainly clear’

Avoid wearing patterned clothing or other detail on your clothing, especially on the upper half of the body, because it will shorten the attention span of the person with whom you are speaking.

Asking people to change

People don't like to change. People are most likely to change when:

- you are able to demonstrate how your request is an extension of their values, self image, or prior actions
- others they respect have already done something similar – not when you are asking them to do something 'new.'

Deepen their commitment before you ask something of someone

The more time a person has spent on a project, the less likely they are to withdraw. Further, the more actions people take on behalf of a belief, the more intensely they will believe it.

The best question you can ask to show respect

'Tell me more about that?' Ask this versatile question when you want to strengthen a relationship. Such situations might include:

- when you are spitting mad and need to cool down
- when you have a blank mind and want to re-group
- when you want to make the other person more committed to what you and they are discussing.

Don't try to deduce other people's intentions from your own fears.

Dealing with anger

Anger can be a cover up for fear. A man may believe it is more appropriate to show anger than the fear that he really feels. Anger can cover up hurt. Better to attack or defend than to show vulnerability. Getting angry helps us to:

- set limits where appropriate
- get our needs met
- get things off our chest
- be assertive
- influence or change others
- discover what is beneath our anger, e.g. hurt

- understand and accept other people's anger

When in an angry situation, it is a good idea to try and reduce the feelings of anger so that you can begin to solve the problem together. What you do is:

- recognise the anger you are picking up in the other person, e.g. 'I can see you are angry about this'
- use listening skills to hear what the other person needs to say before moving onto problem solving
- admit, if appropriate, the possibility that you might have contributed to the problem
- express your desire to solve the problem actively, e.g. 'Let's work this out together'
- get the angry person to calm down, e.g. 'Let's sit down and talk about this'.

Questions you can ask yourself with coping with negative behaviour:

- Do I have the requisite skills to cope with another's negative behaviour?
- Do I need to overcome my mental barrier to other people's negative behaviour?
- Am I managing my anxiety through task-orientated inner dialogue?
- Am I clear on what I need to say?
- What is my contribution to creating the negative situation?
- How defensive am I being?
- Is it worth being assertive?
- Am I backing up my words with the right verbal and non-verbal language?

Everyone needs to feel heard before they'll listen

Managing your anger

Anger is part of our emotional spectrum of self-expression but is all too often either inappropriately expressed, e.g. via aggression, manipulation or blame or denied altogether and stuffed inside never to see the light of day.

Repressed anger can make us defensive, resentful, anxious, depressed, sad, shallow and judgmental. In the long term, it could affect the immune system and make us ill. As with many of our feelings, the way we learn to deal with anger comes via early conditioning. So how we observed role models such as parents deal with anger would affect how we deal with anger as an adult. Gender issues can also affect how we deal with anger. For example, it is traditionally okay for men to show anger and we may expect aggression to come more from men than from women. Many women have a problem with anger, because, traditionally, it hasn't been 'proper' for a woman to express her anger.

Anger needs to be managed effectively and not denied or projected. You can begin to manage your anger through:

- examining what has led you to carry around so much frustration
- striving to increase your threshold for getting angry
- breaking the causes of your frustration down into bite size pieces
- analysing it to see if there isn't some other way you could react to it
- asking yourself how you could react differently to these issues
- making an action plan to change what you can change
- catching yourself when you feel your anger boiling up.

Other ways you could manage your anger include:

- developing an inner arena for expressing anger

  Have a dialogue with your inner parts. Ask yourself what hurt is behind this anger.
- separating your projections from the other person's stuff
- expressing anger physically and safely

  You could punch a cushion, tear up some old magazines or newspapers, do physical exercise or have a good shout to yourself.
- getting your anger out into the open

  Externalise it. You can do this to the person concerned or

if not, try writing it out. Keep on expressing your anger until you reach the underlying feelings or issues.

Keep cool under fire by keeping your bottom line on top of your mind

How we express anger is affected by the negative beliefs we might have about anger.

- I must not make a fool of myself.
- I must always win.
- Others might think I'm pushy if I'm angry.
- Others might not understand my point of view.
- I must be rational all the time.
- I might get out of control if I get angry.
- Others might reject me if I get angry.
- Women shouldn't get angry.
- I must be nice.
- Others might think I'm uptight.
- People won't like me if I get angry.

Developing *task-orientated inner dialogue* is an effective tool in managing anger. Task-orientated inner dialogue is about taking control of our thought processes in relation to how we deal with our own behaviour and the behaviour of others. Actually becoming aware of our thoughts is little like getting hold of air. We tend to be aware of our feelings (vague or intense) and we may be conscious of what causes us to react or behave as we do in response to our feelings. But we can be blissfully ignorant of how our thought processes gives rise to our feelings and behaviours – and more importantly, how we can affect our thought process, for good or bad.

Events Feelings Thoughts

Up until now you may only have been aware of **E** and **F**. However what happens at **T** can be critical, not only for how angry you are because of **E**, but also in regard to how rationally you handle the situation. You can influence **F** by learning to think more realistically at **T**.

Task-orientated inner dialogue can be used before, during and after an event. For example a work colleague keeps using your work area as a dumping ground for their work even after repeated requests for them not to do so. You are going to say something yet again with the comment that you will be putting his work on the floor the next time he puts it on your desk:

Before	Keep calm, remember what I am going to achieve.
During	I am in control. Stick to what I am going to do.
After	Even though the situation is not completely resolved, I'm glad I'm learning to cope without getting aggressive.

There are two kinds of pain: pain of risk and pain of regret

Managing conflict

The art of resolving conflict is to help both parties win something. The basics of conflict management include:

- knowing that conflict can lead to a catalyst for better ideas
- acceptance that conflict is inevitable
- helping parties in conflict maintain self esteem
- digging out hidden agendas
- ensuring both sides see what is in a compromise for them

The first person to experience a conflict rising usually has the greatest opportunity to influence whether the conflict will escalate. A lot happens in those first few moments when people realise the possibility of loss (and every conflict represents a perceived potential loss of some kind). They can lower their guard in an attempt to foster a positive response to the other person. They can act in an open manner in order to find a compromise as things unfold. On the other hand, they can close up and look for more signs of disagreement. The second person in the situation can also use that pivotal point to stay open, even if the first person has already acted, but the second peron's actions will have less effect in the situation.

Suppose you are the first person to experience a conflict arising. You feel vulnerable and instinctively put your guard up. Because you are signalling that your position is weak, you are unwittingly guiding the energy of the ensuing disagreement to your most vulnerable areas. That is why, in that pivotal moment, your choice towards remaining open serves not only to move you toward eventual resolution, but also to protect you. Instead of following your natural instinct to look for more bad signs and prepare to defend yourself or retaliate, you will find it natural to stay aware and open. You will then gain more insight into the motivation and real meaning of the other person's actions.

In conflict we usually get more intense about what we don't want, rather than what we do want. We simply react – we don't choose how we want to act. By so doing, we give our power away by letting others determine our behaviour. It's always more productive to be proactive, to see how you can clear the air. If you steady yourself and decide to be active rather than reactive, you will be satisfied with the results and the ensuing relationships.

TIP BOX ♀⇆♂

MEN AND WOMEN COMMUNICATING WITH EACH OTHER

The following is a brief summary of four key steps in resolving conflict:

Step 1: In a moment of real or imagined confrontation, we escalate into a negative reaction. At such moments, we need to slow down the process and seek clarity by asking what we want. By thinking about your own needs, you blank out the resentment of the other side.

Step 2: Ask yourself: What is this other side's greatest need? By taking the time for this step, you slow down the pace of the discussion.

Step 3:	Listen to the other side and demonstrate to them that you have heard their concerns. This is often the most crucial time in a conflict, when your actions can either spark escalation or initiate a cooling off period.
Step 4:	When you propose a solution, prove that you are fair, by addressing the other person's interests first. Describe, in their language, how they can benefit. Then you can discuss the benefits of such a resolution to yourself as well.

You have come up with a proposal you think is fair to all parties. Before you speak about your own needs, you have addressed their needs first and worked through whatever obstacles that have surfaced. Now it's time to make a firm offer. Don't talk before you are prepared to reach agreement. If you start talking with the other person before you are ready to reach an agreement, you could wind up with less than you want. Be sure you have got what you want out of the situation and that the other person has felt heard. When presenting your proposal, make sure your tone, gestures and language show that you have good intentions. Don't raise your important points at the beginning of the discussion, nor at the end of the discussion. Waiting until the end can close off some of the best options for trade-offs. Reach agreement on your key items before you make any gesture toward finalising agreement. Ask another, mutually respected person to mediate if necessary. A fair and neutral witness can make everyone involved in a conflict feel safer and more heard especially when it's necessary to review items over which you have become deadlocked.

Be flexible to keep the momentum going towards a resolution. Observe how the others are reacting to you and your proposal. Stay flexible so that you can correct yourself and shift gears to make the situation to feel safer and fairer. If feelings seem to be escalating or the other person appears to be shutting down, ask for suggestions and express your willingness to look at other options.

It's important to acknowledge the participation of others. Listen and thoroughly consider other people's opinions at the moment they are presented. If you disagree immediately or counter with another suggestion, reactions will remain hardened long after this particular discussion. Mention that you respect the people who are important to the other side. Praise specific contributions the others have made and let them know you appreciate their efforts.

These seven steps progress from how you might want to begin an effort to resolve differences to how you'd want to complete that effort. Remember to prepare by writing down your goal before taking your first step:

Establish a healthy context Plan and select the right time, place, and atmosphere to negotiate. Agree to ground rules, if necessary, so both parties feel safe and able to speak openly.

Tap into motivation Mutual motivation is prerequisite to effective negotiation. If they have a positional or situational power advantage, appeal to their self-interest (match their values) to motivate them to join you at the negotiation table and grant power to the conversation. If you have more positional or situational power, temporarily suspend that privilege to empower the other party through inclusion. Share the commodities of power so they actively participate in getting to an agreement. Be direct and forthcoming. Speak plainly. People use power differently:

- accommodators give it up
- passive avoiders hold onto interpersonal power
- collaborators go for power with others, or 'shared power.'
- authoritarians use power over others

Remember your goal Before the conversation begins, ask yourself 'What do I want?' If what you want is likely to be unacceptable to the other person then ask yourself 'What would it do for me if I had that?' Be clear about how you'd know if you achieved your desired outcome.

Discover their goal Build rapport as you gather information about what they want. Be curious and interested. Focus first on understanding and defining any problems or issues, then shift to pinpointing their priorities and interests. Ask 'What would that do?' 'how,' and 'when' questions. Avoid 'why.'

Accept and validate their view Accepting it doesn't mean you agree with it or obligate you to share stated interests. Before asking them to understand your view, make sure you understand and can verify exactly how it is for them. Surface any 'Yes, but – ' resistance. Match and mirror to get to the heart of any issues.

Build a bridge Use what you've learned to highlight areas where you agree. Identify your shared concerns against your shared separation. Shift out of 'you against me' and into 'us against the problem.' Lead toward a mutual understanding of 'what we both want.' Moving with any resistance you encounter, propose possible creative alternatives, 'What if I ..., would you ...?' to clarify conditions of satisfaction. Brainstorm several options that would satisfy mutual interests. Two useful questions are, 'What would it take ... (to satisfy both our concerns)?' and 'How might we work it out so that your needs and my needs are both met?' This will open up a variety of ways to reach agreement.

Walk across the bridge Collaborate in selecting the one, best alternative to satisfy shared interests. You'll know you're on the right track when one of you says, 'Which one of these options would work best for you?' or if someone checks to see if there's anything else to talk about. Close the session by verifying understandings and agreements reached, including any further action, inquiry or follow-up steps. Recognise and appreciate cooperation as well as clear boundaries.

Three strategies for handling difficult workplace situations

1. Avoid it

For most garden-variety 'difficulties' (see above), by far the easiest option is avoidance. If you don't have to interact with this person on that topic, why torture yourself trying to get a result that just throws petrol on the fire? If possible, make the difficult behaviour irrelevant. Focus instead on what they're good at besides pushing your buttons. What are their useful strengths? How could you build your relationship around those strengths and bypass the rest?

2. Neutralise your reaction

Your ability to change the situation or change their behaviour depends entirely on your skill at persuasion and negotiation. If you've already tried the direct approach and no dice, the second easiest way is probably to change your reaction to their weirdness. What could you do (or not do) that would keep your buttons from being pushed? For some behaviour, this may be asking a lot. The situation may be simply unacceptable to you.

It is when your reaction is completely justified and still drains your energy that it would be to your advantage to depersonalise and neutralise. Then you can stand there and let them poke around for the former button (the one that used to 'hook' you), and you'll see them looking confused because you're just not going there any more. Being neutral in your reaction is different from approving or liking their behaviour – it simply means that whatever they do, it doesn't faze you. Owning your reaction allows you to become less attached to changing a situation over which you may have no control. Instead, give them a mirror, not an adversary – give nothing to push up against. And if all else fails, try bringing in a neutral third party to assist.

3. Change their behaviour

This third approach – getting them to agree to change – is often the toughest. Why? There's a paradox: the stronger your reaction to their behaviour (that is, the more you get hooked and bothered by it), the harder it is for them to change of their own free will. The more it bothers you, the more it will be in your self-interest for them to change, but what's in it for them? It doesn't usually wash both ways. For example, let's say that to you it's rude, disrespectful and inconsiderate for a co-worker to keep arriving late for meetings; but for them, they may just be arriving when they arrive. If you bring it up, they say, 'Like, what's the big deal?' The 'big deal' is that until you negotiate an agreement that has them bought in to changing, use approaches 1 & 2. If you can't free yourself from needing them to change, in effect, it becomes more your problem than theirs. Do not take on false responsibility. If you can bring the issue to them in a way that they actually let it in, you'll prevent a power struggle.

☞ **Connect with others through what they most value**

TIP BOX ♀⇆♂

MEN AND WOMEN COMMUNICATING WITH EACH OTHER

Four steps to conflict resolution:

1 Tell yourself the truth

We humans build a wall around ourselves, a defence system that clicks into operation whenever we feel affronted in any way. In a moment of confrontation, either real or imagined, we escalate into the hottest negative reaction we can summon. At such moments, we need to slow down the process and seek personal clarity by asking the important question: What do we want? What's our bottom line?

2 Reach out to the other side

Ask yourself these questions. What is this other side's greatest need? What is most important to them? These questions are particularly important if the other side doesn't know their greatest need.

3 Listen attentively to the other side

Listen to the other side and demonstrate to them that you have heard their concerns. Proper respect must be shown at all times, You must mean it. Attitude and words must be respectful and responsive. Power plays will not work at this stage, or later on for that matter. This is often the most crucial time in a conflict, when your actions can either spark escalation or initiate a cooling off period. Don't rush or push now. The more you dislike the other side, the more time and effort you must summon to prove that you are indeed listening, that you are aware of their needs.

4 Prove you are fair

When you propose a solution, prove that you are fair, by addressing the other person's interests first. Describe, in their language, how they can benefit. Then you can discuss the benefits of such a resolution to yourself as well. This is a way of showing proper respect.

Nine approaches for offering your solution

1 Picture each person benefiting in some way

You have come up with a proposal you think is fair to all parties and have shaped your offer so that everyone will see it in the best light possible. Before you speak about your own needs, you have addressed their needs first and worked through whatever obstacles or power issues that have surfaced. Now it's time to make a firm offer. However, in the real world even the best proposal won't go through if it is presented in a way people can't accept. Your manner of presenting your proposal will be more important than its solid core.

There are ways to sabotage a good offer. Present it with open contempt for the other side. Give in to your fear that it won't be accepted. Act in anger or with animosity. Bully others or play king of the mountain.

2 You are emotionally ready to settle

Check your heart and your mind before you open your mouth to seek closure to the conflict.

3 Demonstrate continued good will

At the beginning of conflict, we look for signals from others that tell us how they will act. Later we use these signals as a screen through which we view their actions. So when presenting your proposal, make sure your initial tone, gestures and language show that you have good intentions. Continue to be congenial, specifically because this could be the state when you get more impatient, restless or judgmental as you become tired of the process and the other side. You might try to minimise your defensiveness.

4 Don't leave your most important points for last

Don't raise your important points at the beginning of the discussion, nor at the end of the discussion. Waiting until the end can close off some of the best options for trade-offs. Reach agreement on your key items before you make any gesture toward finalising agreement. When the other side avoids discussion of their most important needs, their avoidance will eventually impede progress toward resolution.

5 Bring out the other's better sides

Orient yourself so that you will look for the other side's more positive traits.

6 Demonstrate your own best traits

People are more inclined to be willing to resolve a conflict with someone they consider fair than with someone they like, but don't trust.

7 Ask another, mutually respected person to mediate when necessary

A fair and neutral witness can make everyone involved in a conflict feel safer and more heard, especially when it's necessary to review items over which you have become deadlocked. This person may be a friend, colleague, or a professional mediator. It doesn't matter as long as the person chosen by both sides has the training and strength of character to stay focused on the solution. It's also wise to have a third party act as witness to your final agreement. It's an extra bit of insurance – sometimes the other side may not live up to the agreement, and if there is a witness, it's harder to avoid making commitments.

8 Stay flexible

Be flexible to keep the momentum going towards a resolution. This flexibility also will restore the momentum where you have gone off track. Observe how the others are reacting to you and your proposal. Stay flexible so that you can correct yourself and shift gears to make the situation to feel safer and fairer. If feelings seem to be escalating or the other person appears to be shutting down, ask for suggestions and express your willingness to look at other options. If you appear to grow more rigid, even if the other side is doing it too, the others will become wary, and suspicious of all your future suggestions.

9 Honour everyone else's role in coming to terms

It's important to acknowledge the participation of others. Listen and thoroughly consider other people's opinions at the moment they are presented. If you disagree immediately or counter with another suggestion, reactions will remain hardened long after this particular discussion. Acknowledge the respect you feel for the others involved. Speak to the relationship you have built. Mention that you respect the people who are important to the other side. Praise specific contributions the others have made and let them know you appreciate their efforts. Make sure that the other side will share your satisfaction in coming to agreement. It's very important that the resolution appears to be arrived at together.

Because we respond more strongly to the negative actions of people for whom we have strong feelings than to those of strangers, allow yourself more time to get back in balance in these cases

Team Building

The purpose of a team is the creation of synergy. This is where the sum of the whole is larger than the sum of each part (individual). Teams are needed when:

- there is uncertainty about a project and you need to share the problems and solutions
- there is a real need for people to work together
- you are experiencing rapid changes
- you are dealing with a problem where nobody knows the answer.

The concept of team roles was 'invented' by Meredith Belbin, one of the foremost experts on team dynamics and is the Visiting Professor at the Centre for Leadership Studies, University of Exeter. Team roles fall into two categories:

1 Their specialist role or responsibility
2 Their team role

Team roles:

Thinker	creative, critical, need for acknowledgement
Organiser	can turn ideas into workable plans, disciplined, efficient, methodical, slow to adopt
Implementer	dutiful, organiser, hard working, disciplined, resistant to change
Plant	unorthodox, serious, imaginative, knowledgeable, problem solver, not too practical
Supporter	team player, concerned with team unit, helpful and supportive to others, mild, diplomatic, dislike confrontation, adapter rather than changer
Specialist	self-starting, provides key knowledge and skills, can be too focused

Chair	calm, self confident, extrovert, dominant, strong sense of objectives, organiser, non-aggressive, can clarify aims of team, not particularly creative
Charismatic player	a salesperson, emotional, insecure, tends to see themselves through the eyes of others
Shaper	highly strung, outgoing, dynamic, lots of drive, prone to irritation and impatience, impulsive, competitive, domineering, concerned with getting things done, intolerant, outgoing, challenging
Entertainer	a performer, a clown, someone who is humorous and who always has something to say
Rescuer	the person who mediates and balances, caring, nurturing
Ideas person	serious minded, unorthodox, imaginative, inclined to disregard practical details
Investigator	enthusiastic, communicative, enjoys exploring new potential, responds to challenge, curious, over-optimistic, loses interest quickly
Dominator	leader, competitive, motivated by a need to be in control
Evaluator	prudent, unemotional, hard headed, lacks inspirations, likes to stick to the rules, identifies with facts and figures, objective, analytical, calm, dependable, can be disparaging
Team worker	social, sensitive, responds to people and situations, promotes team spirit, indecisive at moments of crisis
Traditionalist	tends to identify with a cause, motivated by insecurity and a need to belong
Completer	orderly, conscientious, anxious, perfectionist, worrier, reluctant to let go, good at meeting deadlines, analytical, pays attention to detail

You know team-building is working when:

- feelings are expressed
- success and failure are shared
- conflict is worked through
- objectives are clear
- people work for each other and a higher (company) objective
- good leadership prevails
- information is openly shared
- goals are common to all
- trust is shared
- people help each other

There are many facets to team leadership. An effective team leader will use a mixture of the following typical roles:

Roles	**Purpose**
Executive	sets standards and determines objectives
Controller	organises team output using individual strengths
Coach	develops individual skills
Supporter	provides support and guidance to individuals
Planner	decides how team should reach its goal
Figurehead	focus for team identity
Communicator	provider of direction and information and to listen
Representative	interface between team and outside
Exemplar	stands as a model for the team and leads by example
Recruiter	selects suitable members for the team
Involver	empowers team to become involved in it's processes
Resource manager	uses all available resources to achieve the objectives of the team
Visionary	communicates a vision of the future to the team

TIP BOX ♀⇆♂

MEN AND WOMEN COMMUNICATING WITH EACH OTHER

Teams led by good leaders are ones which:

- have individuals who are allocated tasks they are best suited to
- work to a common objective
- are motivated to do the best they can
- are able to understand their objectives
- are able to understand how the objectives fit in with organisational objectives
- have individuals who know what the team is about and their individual roles within it
- have individuals who support each other
- are prepared to go the extra mile.

Mentoring Others

The concept of mentoring comes from Greek mythology. In Homer's Odyssey, Mentor was the teacher of Telemachus, the son of Odysseus. But Mentor was more than a teacher. Mentor was half-God and half-man, half-male and half-female, believable and yet unreachable. Mentor was the union of both goal and path, wisdom personified (Daloz, 1983). Today, some 3500 years later, mentoring relationships are still valued. Increasingly, mid-career professionals seek mentors when they wish to advance in the profession.

TIP BOX ♀⇆♂

MEN AND WOMEN COMMUNICATING WITH EACH OTHER

The most effective mentor:

- is a confidant, advisor, teacher, guide and coach
- wants to share their knowledge, skill and experience with those they mentor in a non-competitive way
- offers support, challenge, patience and enthusiasm while they guide others to new levels of competence
- exposes the recipients of their mentoring to new ideas, perspectives and standards, and to the values and norms of the profession
- are more expert in terms of knowledge but view themselves as equal to those they mentor
- are considered by peers to be experts in the field and demonstrate superior achievement through their work
- are enthusiastic about their field and continue to update their background in the field

- listen to and communicate effectively with others
- recognise excellence in others and encourage it
- are able to empathise with others and understand their views
- enjoy intellectual engagement and like to help others
- are sensitive to the needs of others and generally recognise when others require support, direct assistance or independence
- exercise good judgement in decisions concerning themselves and the welfare of others.

Establishing a positive mentoring relationship is very much like establishing any valued human relationships, but has the added dimension of being professional in nature. Both parties need to have a desire to understand the values and expectations of the other person, and to respect and become sensitive to one another's feelings and needs. They are responsible for offering support and challenge to the recipient of their mentoring while the recipient strives to fulfil the profession's expectations.

Healthy mentoring relationships are organic rather than static in nature. They change because the purpose of the relationship is to enable the recipient to acquire new knowledge, skill, and standards of professional competence. The perceptions of both members of the relationship evolve as the recipient's performance evolves to new levels of competence under the mentor's guidance and support.

One way to view the evolutionary nature of mentoring relationships is to think of them in terms of stages of development:

Stage 1:	The mentor and recipient become acquainted and clarify their common interests, shared values and professional goals.
Stage 2:	The mentor and recipient communicate initial expectations and agree upon some common procedures and expectations as a starting point.

Stage 3:	Gradually, needs are fulfilled. Objectives are met. Professional growth takes place. New challenges are presented and achieved. This stage may last for months or years.
Stage 4:	The mentor and recipient redefine their relationship as colleagues, peers, partners and/or friends.

In the exploratory stages, individuals who are contemplating a mentoring relationship need to look for:

- a degree of eagerness have a mentoring relationship
- similarity in personal styles: gregarious and spontaneous vs. low-key and reflective
- similarity of expected professional assignments and responsibilities
- similarity in preference for nurture vs. autonomy when establishing expectations for support
- similar professional qualification route, study history and previous experience.

Mentors need to offer their protégés challenges that stimulate professional growth and new levels of expertise. When the amount of challenge is well matched to the mentee's readiness for growth, the tasks become motivating. Challenges that are not matched well with the individual's level of development can create feelings of being unable to cope. Then, rather than producing growth, the challenge may lead to feelings of failure. It is important for mentors to become sensitive to the growth needs of those to whom they mentor, and attempt to offer challenges for their protégé's professional development. Some mentors develop mentoring plans to help maintain optional levels of challenge for the protégé. The primary function of which is to focus on the developmental nature of becoming a professional and to establish mileposts, which will guide and serve as reminders that the recipient is growing in knowledge and skill.

Trust is an important component in the mentoring relationship and includes qualities such as:

assertiveness	reliability	genuineness
dependability	keeping of promises	consistency
trust	loyalty	honesty
fairness	openness	just behaviour
accepting behaviour	caring	support
co-operation	generosity	kindness
keeping of confidences		

The new world of mentoring is about personal growth and development rather than about promotions and plums. And it's more about learning than power. In the old style of mentoring, the best relationships between protégés and mentors were built on commonalities. Everyone knows what an old-style mentor looked like: someone who had a little grey hair and an air of wisdom – a seasoned executive who was several promotions ahead of you. In the new world of mentoring, however, the ideal mentor is impossible to visualise – it could be anyone from anywhere inside or outside of the organisation.

Get creative about how you set up mentoring groups. You could have a mentoring quad, with two mentors and two mentees, or a mentoring circle, with two mentors and from 6 to 10 mentees.

At Apple, for example, the company's women took the initiative in 1994, when Apple scaled back its mentoring programme, its formal staff development, and its diversity activities. A few determined women, including Subhana Ansari, 47, decided that if Apple would not bring mentoring to them, they would bring mentoring to Apple. Ansari, an area administrator, approached other women at Apple with a proposal: with no funding, no support, and no materials, Ansari and other volunteers would build a formal mentoring program in a matter of weeks, starting in March 1996. The classes, which ran for six weeks every Tuesday afternoon, attracted 20 people – 15 women and 5 men – and taught them how to recruit their own mentors. Two people dropped out, but the remaining 18 all had mentors by the fourth week of class. Within four months after the programme was completed, six of the group's members had been promoted. The mentoring programme helped its participants reach new career heights.

Procter & Gamble has created a breakthrough 'reverse mentoring' programme to tutor senior executives about issues facing women. And it's not just men who benefit from the mentoring-in-reverse program. Deb Henretta, 37, the leader of P&G's advancement of women task force, learned from her younger 'reverse mentor' about false assumptions that were affecting young female staff members. 'At P&G, we used to discuss issues of 'work-family balance,'' says Henretta. 'By labelling it that way, we didn't acknowledge that single people had life commitments outside the company.' One measure of the programme's success: P&G has vastly improved its retention rate of talented women. In 1991, the advertising division was losing twice as many women as men. Since the launch of several mentoring initiatives in 1994, the rates have evened out.

It's not about a mentoring relationship. It's about a mentoring mentality. You don't need a single mentor who you keep throughout your career. What you need is a mind-set that allows you to learn from those around you, no matter who they are.

APPENDIX

Diversity Training

You are not looking at diversity training because it is the right thing to do. You are looking at diversity training because your employees and your customers demand it. Corporate diversity efforts are about money, business, and the bottom-line. Here are some preliminary questions you should be asking your employees

- What does diversity mean to you?
- What are our strengths as an organisation with respect to diversity? What are we doing well?
- What could be improved?
- What are your expectations for diversity initiatives and activities that promote a more inclusive work environment?
- What are the professional benefits to you?
- What are the personal benefits to you?

Here are some ideas for information you could gather and review when assessing your corporate culture today and where it needs to be in the future:

Customer surveys: What do your customers say about you (recently and over time)? What do they say about your marketing, sales, and customer retention efforts?

Recruitment: Whom are you recruiting and who are you not? Do you conduct structured group interviews? If you are recruiting through one-on-one interviews, are you getting more people who look just like you or 'remind me of me?' What is your definition of the best candidate?

Attrition rate:	What are the attrition rates of women and minorities as compared to other groups? At what rate are different groups of people entering your workforce (attrition v. recruitment rate)? How does it compare across men, women, race, etc.? Look at data over time, is it improving?
Exit interviews:	Why are people leaving? What are they saying? Who is leaving and who is not?
Attitude surveys:	Have you conducted any attitude surveys in the last year or in the last several years? What did these surveys tell you? What are people saying?

You could form an ad-hoc diversity team or steering committee of employees representative of the whole organisation and delegate these tasks. Without this data, you can't make a serious business case for instituting diversity training and other corporate-wide initiatives to create and promote a more inclusive work environment in your organisation.

Anyone who has ever attempted to conduct diversity training in organisations of any size has encountered such data collection. No matter how good the material, how engaging the exercises, how skilled the group process techniques, there is one obstacle even the most experienced and skilled facilitator cannot overcome – the unexamined negative reactions to the message. All an organisation requires to become jittery about a diversity intervention is to see a few bad evaluations and diversity training becomes the nucleus of all things negative. Often, the resolution is to avoid confronting anything which smacks of diversity, or at least to insure the next facilitator does nothing to disturb the fragile dispositions of future trainees. There seems to be a kind of mass collusion, which militates against attempts to teach value and respect for people's differences. The co-conspirators include:

- diversity professionals who have not prepared clients to engage in a process capable of achieving significant and abiding outcomes
- individuals who are reluctant to explore diversity issues

- organisations who are unclear about diversity goals
- inherited social systems, which unfairly advantage some, and limit others.

> Organisations must be clear about what they are committed to accomplish before launching a diversity awareness and training program. While this may seem clear, it is often the case that they respond to disturbing incidents, e.g. the distribution of deprecating jokes with no clear strategy in mind. Rather than reacting to periodic events, organisations will be better served by thinking strategically about the level of proficiency and understanding required to achieve its diversity goals. Doing so will help to address negative occurrences in the context of an overall diversity framework, and will prove useful in determining appropriate intervention. Thus, the organisation will have the advantage of correlating the chosen intervention to the strategic business purpose that makes it necessary. Employees are better able to understand the strategic reasons requiring their personal involvement. Supervisors are better equipped to explain why employee attendance is requested, and leadership becomes clear about how much time, money, effort and personal presence is required to ensure strategic goals are met.

Diversity training needs to be:

positive	looking to the future
pro-active	talking about shared responsibilities
introspective	internally driven
non-confrontational	holistic and organisation-wide
practical and real world geared	participant cantered
unifying participants	customised and eclectic
client/trainer partnership	skills and knowledge-based

11 reasons why diversity training fails

1. Training is all the organisation is doing. The organisation is not reviewing or scrutinising their recruitment, promotion, leadership development, and business practices.

2. There isn't a formal, inclusive mentoring program in place.

3. Are you a homogeneous company (senior and upper management) marketing and selling to a heterogeneous or diverse marketplace? Or, will a heterogeneous company (your competitor) understand and anticipate the needs of your heterogeneous or diverse marketplace more effectively than you and your homogeneous company?

4. The diversity training has management's support, e.g. resources but not their commitment (management or senior management in particular, does not walk the talk). Management's lack of participation is all the evidence the rest of the organisation needs to resist the training and consider it the next fad.

5. The training being conducted is not custom designed to meet the unique needs of the particular organisation. The training fails because participants were not engaged, not interested, and did not find the training practical, pertinent and compelling.

6. Training is being developed and led solely by external diversity consultants and trainers. The training is thus the consultant's programme and not a programme developed by the employees of the organisation, for the organisation. No ownership or buy-in is solicited and thus none is secured and the programme eventually perishes and the external diversity trainer is the patsy.

7. Internal resources are not formed, developed, and encouraged e.g. internal diversity change co-ordinator. You haven't formed an internal diversity steering committee and haven't trained and developed internal change personnel to 'keep the fires burning.' You have not continued the work once the external diversity trainer has moved on.

8. Diversity training must come from the whole organisation through a diversity steering committee made up of employees from a representative cross-section of the organisation.

9. Diversity training is being done because it is the right thing to do. The organisation does not understand the connection between diversity and the bottom line.

10. Your diversity training had no formal follow-up. Many of the action items had no owners and no one revisited the training. Training alone is not the cure-all panacea. You need to have internally driven initiatives supported by senior management commitment as well as ongoing attention and training from internal as well as external subject matter experts.

11. Your diversity-training programme is awareness-based but provides no skills, no practical, 'hands-on', everyday tools. People are heard saying, 'What am I supposed to do now? I go back to my workplace tomorrow.'

Successful diversity training

- It does not occur in a vacuum and must be supported by other initiatives and activities. Training alone is not the 'cure-all.' A formal mentoring program that includes and encourages all employees to participate is another potential diversity initiative.
- It is thoroughly planned, implemented, and measured for its impact on the organisation.
- It takes on a life of its own. Employees are encouraged to get involved, develop and lead brown-bag discussions, mini-training, and other activities.
- A formal diversity-learning centre is established. Such a centre has books, videos, audiotapes, CD-ROMS, and other learning materials available for all employees when they need such assistance. There is an ongoing and continuous commitment to creating and promoting a more inclusive work environment that values our differences.
- It is supported by sound research. Your organisation is presenting the business rationale, the bottom-line results of doing this work. Also presented are the costs of not doing this work. Your company is doing this work because their future, market share, retention of talent, and performance depend on understanding and anticipating the needs of an increasingly diverse workplace and marketplace.
- it is 'skill-based.' All diversity training is awareness based.
- It ensures transfer of skills from the training room to the workplace. Diversity training should educate and empower all

employees with new skills and tools.

- It is not dependent on a 'saviour.' Do not rely on one person (diversity trainer or manager of diversity) to save the organisation. A steering committee representing the whole organisation must uniformly champion all of the initiatives.
- It is developed through a partnership of internal employees (diversity steering committee) and an external subject matter expert (diversity consultant and trainer).
- It has a senior-level advocate or champion. The champion of the internal diversity steering committee is the MD or CEO of your organisation. He/she participated in workshops where all of the diversity training consultant candidates considered were asked to present and train. You test drove all of the diversity-training contractors and picked the best trainer – not the one that looked best on paper.

Ideas for diversity training workshops

Here are three ideas for diversity workshops, which also offer opportunities for transferable skills training:

Presentation Styles

How receptive is your organisation to differences in style and approach? Does your organisation use different standards in evaluating male and female employees?

Key learning points:

- understanding how cultural style may impact on perceptions of performance
- developing consistency in coaching employees
- avoiding double standards in work
- understanding issues and perceptions of people of different genders
- developing skills to lead diverse employees
- gaining awareness of the pitfalls of conformity

Transferable learning opportunities:

- coaching
- mentoring
- cultural awareness
- change
- communication
- listening
- diversity

Gender Issues and Career Development

Balancing work and family is an issue more women have to cope with than men, and these issues can have a negative impact on women's careers and advancement opportunities. This programme will generate great discussion on gender issues and how to balance career and family. You'll understand the subtleties that can exist in this complex issue, particularly as you look at the different values and styles that conflict in the workforce between women and men from different cultural backgrounds.

Key learning points:

- understanding effective career planning and development
- developing skills to lead diverse employees
- balancing work and family
- understanding the challenges faced by women and those with families
- understanding subtle attitudes toward people with disabilities
- awareness of subtle sexism and racism
- developing retention strategies for women.i

Transferable learning opportunities:

- listening
- building trust
- communication
- career planning
- diversity awareness
- work/family issues
- recruitment and retention of women

The inclusive vs. non-inclusive organisation

Many times, new employees, especially those who are different, are not properly introduced and mentored into the organisation. In this scenario, your audience will be able to explore the conflicts and potential implications for organisations that fail to have an inclusive, holistic process for mentoring and introductions. Research shows that the first years in a new organisation or organisation can greatly impact the employee's effectiveness and also his or her desire to stay in the organisation. Now you can use this program to develop a dialogue and plan to effectively utilise and develop all employees.

Key learning points:

- understanding the importance of career planning and development
- understanding and preventing stereotypes
- mentoring diverse employees effectively
- including employees in the formal and informal organisational networks
- developing strategies to retain top talent
- communicating effectively on tough issues.

Transferable learning opportunities:

- change
- communication
- listening
- building trust
- mentoring
- diversity awareness
- career planning
- retention of diverse employees
- leadership

If organisations are to evolve into inclusive and valuing environments, they will likely need the assistance of diversity professionals from within, or outside of, the organisation. Diversity specialists have a responsibility to help clients understand the depth and complexity of the issues. Their advice should include detailed discussions of the kinds of organisational support required to overcome the negative reactions, which inexorably arise. They should help organisations understand the obstacles they are likely to encounter, and more importantly, how to overcome them. This is a task made more difficult by the tendency of clients to want to approach diversity training in much the same manner as they deal with other concerns, and by the tendency of many diversity specialists to allow them to do so.

Dealing with Sexual Harassment

Harassment is any form of unwanted and unwelcome behaviour, which may range from mildly unpleasant remarks to physical violence. Harassment is termed sexual harassment if the unwanted behaviours are linked to your gender or sexual orientation.

The EU definition of sexual harassment is 'unwanted conduct of a sexual nature or other conduct based on sex, affecting the dignity of men and women at work'.

The principal areas of UK law relating to harassment comprise:

- Sex Discrimination Act 1975: discrimination on the grounds of sex by dismissing an employee or submitting them to 'any other detriment'
- Protection from Harassment Act 1996: harassment and stalking
- Criminal Justice & Public Order Act 1994: intentional harassment [text?] for causing another person harassment, alarm or distress by using threatening, abusive or insulting words or behaviour
- Criminal law of assault
- Race Relations Act 1976: ditto on racial grounds
- Disability Discrimination Act 1995: ditto on grounds of disability

Sexual harassment might apply to lesbians or gay men as well as heterosexual women and men. The first case which came to British justice was in 1986, when a female laboratory technician took her company to court over sexual harassment (and won). That was when the way opened for other women to take cases under the Sex Discrimination Act. Sexual harassment does not have to involve sexual desire. But if the comments or behaviour reflect your gender and makes you feel uncomfortable then it becomes sexual harassment.

The workplace is taking on a more democratic structure that encourages participation by all workers in a team environment. As the workforce becomes more diverse, recognising and capitalising on the differences between men and women will become more important. Successful companies and managers will learn that men and women work, think and communicate differently. The successful manager will embrace those differences and apply the benefits of each style of communication to improve their division of the company. The workplace does not have to be perfect. It is appropriate to tell jokes, tease, and have fun as long as the working environment remains safe for everybody.

Sexual harassment in the work environment has become a major issue in the last thirty years. If someone is harassing another person, that behaviour should not be tolerated. In the working environment, men and women are equally being sexually harassed by either sex (Nelson: *A New Era*). In addition, the term sexual harassment is encompassing the rudeness of the client/customer to the worker.

> When an individual thinks of sexual harassment, one usually thinks of a male→female arrangement, whereby the male is the harasser and the female is being harassed. In the last ten to fifteen years, however, those assumptions have been rapidly reversing. The current definition of harassment includes same-sex harassment as well as female→male harassment.

Many corporations and businesses have produced written documents that prohibit sexual harassment within their organisation. Even strictly written documentation prohibiting sexual harassment has a hard time stopping the activities. If a business formulates the rules against harassment but takes no action to implement the rules within the organisation, the perception of individuals may evolve into an attitude in which harassment is acceptable in an employee's mind.

Broadly speaking, sexual harassment is more common for women than for men and tends to occur where there is a major difference in status between individuals within the workplace. The following behaviours can indicate sexual harassment:

- the boss who promises promotion in return for sexual favours or demotion if not complied with
- unnecessary body contact
- the office junior given a difficult time by the adult males or females in the office
- offensive pin-ups
- degrading remarks
- crude comments about personal appearance
- the woman manager given a difficult time by a male subordinate
- sexual jokes
- the male group who ridicule a women entering a male-dominated workplace
- the female group who ridicule a man entering a female-dominated workplace

There are a number of reasons why sexual harassment occurs. Primarily it occurs from negative and ignorant beliefs such as:

- the perception that women or men are sex objects due to media presentation and role model behaviour
- bullies can enjoy tormenting people weaker than themselves
- males or females should stick together and prove themselves by undermining the opposite gender
- men are superior and women are inferior
- women should be submissive not equal
- that lesbians and gay men are inferior to heterosexual men and women
- men have the workplace as their domain.

The most prominent of the new age complaints are those cases involving men harassed by female supervisors. In most harassment cases, whether the assailant is male or female, the main motive is not romance but power. Today, women hold a growing percentage of all managerial and supervisory positions and are increasingly inclined to play the power game. The main dilemma a man faces when he is harassed by a woman is that he is more inclined to be embarrassed and is reluctant to speak out for fear that he will be humiliated and ostracised by his co-workers. Male victim cases can sometimes present problems due to society's stereotypes of women and men. Our mental models maintain the assumption that males find sexual advances from women non-threatening and even enjoyable.

We must take all complaints seriously or we will lose creditability. Procedures for dealing with harassment cases should be consistent, regardless of gender or status. However, companies should still take into account the victim's personality and the circumstances. They should treat every complaint confidentially, investigate each thoroughly and take appropriate and immediate disciplinary action.

Signs of sexual harassment

- compliments with sexual overtones
- office or locker room pin-ups
- unwelcome physical conduct or sexual advances
- suggestive remarks
- teasing or taunting of a sexual nature
- continual use of offensive language
- bragging about sexual prowess
- sexual bantering
- comments about the way people look which they find demeaning
- indecent remarks
- questions about people's sex life
- sexual demands by a member of your own or the opposite sex

Women and men have a right not to be subjected to sexual harassment at work. The Sex Discrimination Act (SDA) makes it unlawful for employers in Great Britain to treat a woman less favourably than a man (or vice versa) in similar circumstances by subjecting her to a detriment. It is also unlawful to discriminate against an individual undergoing gender reassignment. Sexual harassment itself can amount to less favourable treatment but in many instances it will be accompanied by other forms of unfavourable treatment such as not being recruited, criticism of work, lack of promotion, enforced transfer and ill health or dismissal. You can only take a claim of sexual harassment under the SDA if the sexual harassment you are complaining of took place in work or at a work related function.

A booklet is issued by the Department of Employment called *Sexual Harassment in the Workplace: A Guide for Employers.*

Ideas for training workshops

Here are two ideas for diversity workshops, which also offer opportunities for transferable skills training:

Sexual Harassment

Even with the publicity and information about sexual harassment, many people remain unclear about what sexual harassment is and what to do about it. In addition, many, especially men, believe that sexual harassment has created an uncomfortable, politically correct environment. This scenario explores the issue of sexual harassment in the plant floor and in the office. You will be able to use this programme as a springboard to review your organisation's policy on sexual harassment and discuss the many misconceptions that exist about sexual harassment. It is essential that all employees make the workplace a healthy environment, regardless of gender

Key learning points:

- developing skills to lead diverse employees
- enhancing awareness of sexual harassment at work
- avoiding misconceptions of gender issues
- developing skills to deal with sensitive issues

Transferable learning opportunities:

- communication
- listening
- sexual harassment
- gender issues
- teambuilding

Gender Conflicts in Cross-Cultural Global Communications

You are a female executive travelling to South America. You're meeting with an Argentinian executive who works for your organisation. Jesus gives Alison a warm handshake and puts his hands on her shoulders. He looks her up and down. He says 'Alison, it is so nice to first meet you in person. Your office didn't tell me they were going to send such a beautiful woman. Come in and sit down. It is wonderful to have you in Argentina, just wonderful.' (He pulls out her chair for her). Jesus continues to tell her how beautiful she is and continues to talk about social issues. Alison begins to feel uncomfortable but she tries to cover it up.

How can you tell the difference between possible sexual harassment and or cultural difference? How do different cultures perceive work and life? What is important to them? How do you handle the conflict between UK and Latino perception of women and sexual harassment? How do you build trust and respect across different cultures?

Key learning points:

- understanding areas of difference including styles, time, communication, and male-female work relationships
- developing skills to lead a diverse workforce
- building trust and respect across cultures
- developing enhanced awareness of what defines sexual harassment
- understanding different cultures' approaches to work and life.

Transferable learning opportunities:

- conflict resolution
- communication
- sexual harassment
- teambuilding
- global diversity
- intercultural communication and awareness.

The law

The Acts, which may apply to you if you are subjected to sexual harassment at work, are:

- The Sex Discrimination Act (**www.eoc.org.uk/advice/sh/#sda**)

- The Employment Rights Act **(www.eoc.org.uk/advice/sh/#era**

The codes of practice, which may apply to you if you have been subjected to sexual harassment at work, are:

- The Equal Opportunities Commission's (EOC) code of practice (**www.eoc.org.uk/advice/sh/#eoc**)
- The European Commission's code of practice on the Protection of the Dignity of Women and Men at Work (**www.eoc.org.uk/advice/sh/#ec**)

The Sex Discrimination Act 1975

The Sex Discrimination Act (SDA) makes it unlawful for employers and other organisations to treat women or men less favourably because of their sex in the area of employment. Discrimination can take the following forms:

- **Direct sex discrimination** is less favourable treatment of a woman than a man (or vice versa) because of their sex. Most sexual harassment is direct discrimination, because you are being treated in a way a person of the other sex would not be treated.
- **Indirect sex discrimination** occurs when a condition or requirement is applied equally to both women and men but, in fact, it affects more women than men and is not genuinely necessary. This type of discrimination may only rarely be applicable to sexual harassment.
- **Victimisation.** You must not be treated less favourably compared to others because you acted in good faith to assert your rights under the SDA. You will have a victimisation claim if your employer treats you less favourably than another employee because you have complained of sexual harassment: for example, if your employer dismisses you or does not promote you because of your complaint.

Who is covered by the SDA?

- The SDA covers a broad range of workers including contract workers.

- It applies regardless of length of service in employment and regardless of the number of hours you work.
- It allows you to take a case to an employment tribunal. If your case is successful, you will be awarded compensation for any financial loss you have suffered; an award for injury to feelings can also be made.

To claim sex discrimination

You need to be able to show that:

- you found the behaviour offensive
- the treatment received did constitute sexual harassment
- someone of the opposite sex would not have been treated in this way.

- In cases involving *same sex* sexual harassment, you need to show that the harasser would not have treated a person of the opposite sex in the same way.
- In cases involving harassment because of *gender reassignment*, you need to show your gender reassignment is the reason for the treatment received. The harassment was either sexual in nature such as indecent remarks, questions about your sex life or directed at one sex only compared to the opposite sex.

The Employment Rights Act 1996

If you have one year's service with your employer, you may also have a claim for unfair dismissal/constructive dismissal, in addition to your claim of sex discrimination, if:

- you are dismissed
- you have to resign because you cannot bear to work in your job any longer as a result of the harassment
- you are considering leaving your job because of the harassment or your employer has failed to investigate/take action about your complaints. (Before resigning, it is best to take legal advice.)

There is a three month time limit for taking legal action under the Employment Rights Act.

The Equal Opportunities Commission's (EOC) code of practice on Sex Discrimination

The code of practice makes recommendations to employers, trade unions and other organisations on how to avoid incidents of sex discrimination and victimisation. The code also recommends basic proactive measures that organisations should take in order to help achieve equality between men and women at work. Both aspects of the code should be helpful in any tribunal claim you may make. The EOC recommends all reasonable practical steps should be taken to ensure a standard of conduct/behaviour is observed which prevents members of either sex from being intimidated, harassed or otherwise subjected to unfavourable treatment because of their sex.

The European Commission's (EC) code of practice on the Protection of the Dignity of Women and Men at Work

The European Commission's code recognises sexual harassment as being conduct that undermines the dignity of men and women at work. The Code defines sexual harassment to be unwanted conduct of a sexual nature, or other conduct based on sex affecting the dignity of women and men at work, which include physical, verbal and non-verbal conduct. It states that the conduct of superiors or colleagues is unacceptable if:

- it is unwanted, unreasonable and offensive to the recipient
- the recipient's rejection or submission to the conduct is used explicitly or implicitly as a basis for a decision affecting their job, promotion, training, salary, or any other employment decision
- it creates an intimidating, hostile, or humiliating working environment for the recipient and that such conduct may be in breach of the Equal Treatment Directive.

The European Commission recommends that employers should:

- treat sexual harassment as misconduct and deal with harassers accordingly
- adopt procedures/policies for dealing with sexual harassment
- issue a statement that sexual harassment will not be tolerated
- train all staff in the policies adopted.

What can you do?

If you feel that you have been sexually harassed at work you should follow clear procedures.

- Take some important first steps to make it clear you reject the treatment, and to record what has happened.
- Approach your employer to explain what has been happening to you. Your employer should then take steps to deal with your complaints. They should hold an investigation into your complaint, taking disciplinary action against the harasser, as appropriate, and inform you of the outcome. The investigation should be conducted speedily and objectively. You should not be penalised in any way.
- Go to your trade union to ask for support either with your employer and/or the employment tribunal.
- Contact the police as soon as possible. Sexual assault and some forms of sexual harassment can amount to a criminal offence that may lead to criminal prosecution. You can still make a claim to the employment tribunal whether or not criminal proceedings are taken.
- Seek advice from a solicitor on whether criminal proceedings may be appropriate.
- You can:
  - take your claim to the employment tribunal
  - contact the EOC for further advice
  - go to a Citizens Advice Bureau (CAB) for more advice on your situation. Find your nearest CAB on the National Association of Citizens Advice Bureaux (NACAB) website (**www.nacab.org.uk**)

If you are being sexually harassed at work there are a number of important steps you should take at the outset.

- Starting a journal can help an individual in case the situation terminates in a legal confrontation. The journal should be as specific as possible, citing what happened, where the harassment occurred as well as the date and any witnesses. Another good idea is to write individual feelings in the journal at the point when the harassment occurred, especially if an individual believes that his or her work is suffering from the episode.

- To ask if anyone else has had difficulty with the harasser. Talk to the same gender colleagues – you may find several other people have experienced sexual harassment from the same person. If any of your colleagues are being, ask them to keep a diary, even if they have not reported the problem.
- Another tactic to stop sexual harassment is to confront the harasser directly, but privately. You may ask a trusted colleague or trade union representative to accompany you. A witness will give you moral support and can provide evidence in any grievance or employment tribunal proceedings. The harasser should be informed that his or her behaviour is unacceptable and that the basis of the work environment should be based on a professional work relationship. If the harasser disagrees with an individual's assessment, the best tactic for the harassed individual is to remain calm and specifically repeat the message to the harasser.
- You might prefer to write to the harasser explaining the distress his or her behaviour is causing and asking for it to stop. Say that you will take further action if the harasser persists. Keep a copy of your letter.
- You could bypass the harasser and confer with the harasser's supervisor. This tactic can be used in any situation: whether the harasser is a co-worker or a supervisor. In any case, a supervisor should be involved unless that individual is the harasser, in which case, the individual's supervisor should be involved.
- Consider telling a friend or colleague you trust who will uphold confidentiality. You will feel better if you know you are not alone and this evidence may also help if you decide to take a claim to the tribunal.
- Tell your doctor if you are suffering any symptoms of stress, depression or ill health as a result of the harassment. Obtain a medical report from a doctor, counsellor and or psychologist, which shows that the illness you are suffering from, is as result of the treatment you have received. This will be important if you decide to take a claim to a tribunal

You will need to consider taking your claim to the employment tribunal if:

- you have told the harasser to stop and reported it to your employer but it is still continuing
- the alleged harasser is the owner of the company and there is no one else in the company to complain to
- you are not satisfied with the way your employer handled the investigation or its outcome

Contacting your trade union

You can ask your trade union for support in approaching your manager or employer. They may also be able to attend meetings with you, help if you cannot resolve matters satisfactorily and wish to take a formal grievance, or take your complaint to the employment tribunal. You can ask for help either from a local trade union representative, or by contacting a full-time officer. If you have any difficulties with your local union representative about your claim, contact the district or regional officer who should be able to help. If you still have difficulty then get in touch with your union's national women's officer or equal opportunities officer via your union's head office. In some circumstances, the union may arrange for a lawyer to represent you at a tribunal hearing.

Conciliation through ACAS

ACAS is an independent body with a statutory duty to try to settle cases about employment rights. As soon as ACAS receives a copy of the ET1, your claim is allocated to a conciliation officer. This officer will contact you and the respondent and will offer to conciliate, or attempt to negotiate a settlement, between you. If you and the respondent are willing to accept conciliation, the officer will help you to try to reach a settlement without the need for a tribunal hearing. Conciliation is voluntary so both you and the respondent are free to decline or discontinue ACAS assistance at any stage. The conciliation officer has a duty to be impartial and independent and cannot act as a representative for either party. The officer will explain the tribunal procedure, the relevant law, and the way tribunals have approached similar cases in the past. The officer will also help you to establish the facts of your complaint and to clarify your views. The officer will explain your views to the respondent and the respondent's views to you. It is not the officer's job to form an opinion on the merits of your case, or to express their own views about it. It is not the officer's job to approve or even recommend a particular settlement. It is up to you and the respondent to sort out and agree the terms. It is therefore very important that you have a clear idea of what you will settle for and that you list separately all the items for which you are claiming compensation. If you do agree a settlement, the terms will be drawn up on a COT3 form. This is legally binding on both you and the respondent. If you do not want to accept a settlement, your case will go to the tribunal for a hearing.

Further guidance on making a claim

For further information about how the tribunal system works, phone the Employment Tribunal Enquiry Line on 0845 7959775.

How can I contact the EOC for advice?

- If you live in England, you can telephone or write to an EOC casework officer at: Arndale House, Arndale Centre, Manchester, M4 3EQ. Telephone: 0161 833 9244. You can e-mail on info@eoc.org.uk
- If you live in Wales, the address and telephone number are: Windsor House, Windsor Lane, Cardiff, CF10 3GE. Tel: 02920 343552. You can e-mail on wales@eoc.org.uk
- If you live in Scotland, the address and telephone number are: St Stephens House, 279 Bath Street, Glasgow, G2 4JL. Tel: 0141 248 5833. You can e-mail on Scotland@eoc.org.uk

Bullying in the Workplace

Workplace bullying is the hurtful and repeated mistreatment of workers by their bosses, co-workers or subordinates. It's a pattern of abusive remarks, arbitrary rages or attempts to sabotage a person's work. The most common bullying behaviours can include talking behind people's backs, interrupting people when they are speaking or working, flaunting authority or status, acting in a condescending manner and belittling people's opinions to others. Other behaviours may include the silent treatment, insults, yelling, shouting and staring or abusive e-mail messages (flame mail). People often react to the bully by worrying about a specific incident or future interactions, losing work time while avoiding the bully, being absent or tardy or leaving early and by changing jobs.

The law

There are four main pieces of health and safety law, which are relevant to violence at work. These are:

- **The Health and Safety at Work etc Act 1974**. Employers have a legal duty under this Act to ensure, so far as is reasonably practicable, the health, safety and welfare at work of their employees.
- **The Management of Health and Safety at Work Regulations 1992**. Employers must assess the risks to employees and make arrangements for their health and safety by effective planning, organisation, control, monitoring and reviewing.
- **The Reporting of Injuries, Diseases and Dangerous Occurrences Regulations 1995 (RIDDOR)**. Employers must notify their enforcing authority in the event of an accident at work to any employee resulting in death, major injury or incapacity for normal work for three or more days. This includes any act of non-consensual physical violence done to a person at work.

- **Safety Representatives and Safety Committees Regulations 1977** (a) and **The Health and Safety (Consultation with Employees) Regulations 1996** (b). Employers must inform, and consult with, employees in good time on matters relating to their health and safety. Employee representatives, either appointed by recognised trade unions under (a) or elected under (b) may make representations to their employer on matters affecting the health and safety of those they represent.

All employers should have a policy on harassment and discrimination, which protects both employees and the employer. The motivation is twofold: to provide an atmosphere in which employees can fulfil the duties and obligations of their contract free from harassment and discrimination, and to comply with UK and European law, specifically, the **Sex Discrimination Act (1975), the Race Relations Act (1976)**, and the **Disability Discrimination Act (1996).** The policy needs to state that reprehensible behaviour is not acceptable and provides both a statement to all employees and a recognised and agreed course of action to be taken should any employee behave in an unacceptable manner. Existence and implementation of a policy also means that the employer is much less likely to be involved in employment tribunals and litigation.

Bullying differs from harassment and discrimination in that the focus is rarely based on gender, race, or disability. The focus is often the alleged lack of competence of the bullied person. In reality, the target of bullying is often competent and popular, and the bully is aggressively projecting their own social, interpersonal and professional inadequacy onto their target. The purpose of projection is to avoid facing up to that inadequacy and doing something about it, and to distract and divert attention away from the bully's inadequacies. Bullying is a form of violence; it is aggression expressed psychologically rather than physically.

A policy must state clearly that bullying is a disciplinary offence, which links the behaviour into existing disciplinary procedures. To be effective, the policy must state that confidentiality is guaranteed. The main steps are as follows:

- It's a good idea to ensure that everyone is involved and can contribute to the process from the outset including directors, management, personnel, staff, trade unions, health and safety reps, counselling and welfare department, workers' representatives, etc.
- You can ask staff for their views on bullying with an attitude survey. Surveys returned anonymously are likely to be more reliable. A good source of reliable data comes from exit interviews.
- Keep statistics on staff turnover. This will indicate trouble spots and along with the results of the staff attitude survey will give you hard data with which to measure improvement as your policy takes effect. This information will help convince sceptics, doubters, auditors, shareholders, taxpayers, donors, etc. that this data can be converted into cost.
- Understand bullying through:
    - reading books on workplace bullying and those on related topics of stress, harassment, discrimination, violence, etc
    - attending conferences and events on bullying and build a network of contacts
    - making contact with fellow professionals
    - absorbing information from your professional bodies.
- Share your knowledge of bullying with all employees so that everyone is talking about the same thing. People hate policy documents and official documents. However, they anticipate and welcome news, so, rather than just updating staff handbooks and sending copies of policies to everybody, condense your initiative into a news item in the employer's newsletter.
- Instead of having one policy on harassment, have an overall policy called, say, 'Dignity at Work', which contains an introduction stating the reasons for having this policy etc, then separate chapters on harassment, discrimination, assault and violence, bullying, treatment of minorities, etc, in line with your chosen ethos and emphasis. You can orient it towards equal

opportunities, or diversity, or legalities, or cost, or benefits to employees and business, or whatever you choose. This way, you can update individual sections without having to re-issue the whole policy every time.

NOTE: The phrase '**Dignity at Work**' derives from European law, whereby harassment and discrimination are examples of unacceptable behaviour, which 'affect the dignity of men and women at work'.

- The cost of bullying rarely appears in the accounts. Discover how much bullying is costing you in terms of staff time wasted, staff turnover, sickness absence, poor productivity, low morale, poor customer service, etc. Putting a cost on bullying will convince senior minds, should any persuasion be necessary.
- Ensure that you know how to investigate a case of bullying. Unlike harassment, assault etc, there will be little physical evidence.
- Provide a member of staff to whom anyone who feels they are being bullied can talk. This person must be trained in bullying, harassment, and counselling, and meetings must be guaranteed confidential. The presence of this person will deter genuinely poor performers who are claiming to be bullied from using it as an excuse. It might be appropriate to make it mandatory in your policy for targets to meet this independent person before any action can be taken.
- Provide ongoing training for all staff covering bullying and harassment (bullying awareness, harassment and discrimination issues etc) and how to deal with it (assertiveness, interpersonal skills, confidence and esteem building etc). This might be part of a larger Employee Assistance Programme.

Most policy recommendations suggest a two-tier procedure: an informal stage and then, if the informal stage is not sufficient, a formal stage.

Guidelines for the informal stage

- The person who believes they are being bullied needs to be able to discuss their situation with somebody who is empathic and trained in these issues.
- At this stage, it's essential to identify the type of bullying that has been reported. You will establish this through an informal investigation. The person who undertakes this role must be impartial and fully trained in bullying and investigation techniques specific to bullying.
- Unwitting and organisational bullying can often be defused at this stage without the need to escalate matters to the formal stage. With unwitting bullying, a quiet word or a letter from the target will often be sufficient. The unwitting bully may need assistance, especially if his or her behaviour has deteriorated due to excessive workload or inadequate training or lack of support.
- Whether you make and keep any written records at this stage is a decision for you. You could keep a note on file, which includes a statement that it should only be taken into account if formal or further informal procedures are initiated.
- To counter the target's request that they don't want any action to be taken against the bully at this stage and they don't want it to be investigated, the policy should have a clear statement along the lines that 'the employer is under a legal obligation of a duty of care to provide both a safe place and a safe system of work; any bullying that is reported must be investigated, first informally, and later, if appropriate, formally, in order to comply with this duty of care. This duty of care cannot be derogated.' Derogated means avoided or abdicated or passed to someone else for any reason. The policy must also have a clause stating that victimisation as a result of reporting bullying and harassment will be regarded as a serious breach of discipline and automatically result in a formal investigation, which, if proven, may result in disciplinary action being taken against the perpetrator, which may include dismissal. The policy also needs a clause stating, 'the making of false or

malicious complaints of bullying and harassment will be regarded as a serious disciplinary offence'.

- At the informal stage, should you, the employer, bring the two sides (alleged bully and target) together? It depends on the circumstances and you should be guided by the needs of the target and the results of your own informal investigation. With unwitting bullying, bringing the two sides together may be appropriate, especially if mediation is used.

Guidelines for the formal procedure

- The formal procedure must state clearly in writing what the procedure involves and what the possible outcomes will be. Rights of appeal for both parties should also be made clear at this stage.
- The first step is to find out the facts, so an investigation by a trained investigator is essential. The investigator must be impartial and confidentiality must be guaranteed; with a serial bully, most employees will be too frightened to come forward of their own volition.
- A good starting point is the bully's CV; bullies often lie about their qualifications and experience, or describe it in ambiguous terms, which are misleading. For example 'I undertook a degree course in xxx' may give the impression of holding a degree but may mean, 'I started the course but didn't complete it because I failed the exams'.
- Representation is a grey area with many employers claiming that the person who is the alleged target of bullying is not entitled to representation. Denial of representation is a common tactic by which bullies reveal themselves, therefore any reasonable employer will allow and encourage both parties to have a representative of their choice and without limitation present in all meetings related to the formal procedure. The Employment Rights Act gives employees the legal right to be accompanied during grievance procedures and disciplinary hearings, but only by a union rep or fellow worker; the former often are too involved

with management to be impartial, and the latter are too frightened to come forward. A reasonable employer will go beyond what the law requires and allow the target to be accompanied by a person of his or her own choosing.

If someone's behaviour toward you has gone beyond legitimate work criticism or rare misdeeds, consider taking these steps:

- Get support from family, friends or a counsellor (perhaps through your Employee Assistance Programme). Don't suffer in silence.
- Avoid being alone with the bully.
- Document the behaviour in writing. Be specific. Include its impact on productivity and the bottom line.
- Team up with any co-workers who also are being targeted.
- Determine if any company policies have been violated.
- If you feel comfortable doing so, tell the person bullying you that it bothers you.
- If the worst comes to the worst, consider requesting a transfer for yourself.

Useful resources

AnSer House of Marlow UK. www.anserhouse.co.uk.

Exponents on the development of good diversity/equal opportunity management and practice in the UK from publishing through to training, especially in an advisory capacity.

Angel Productions. 9 Dukes Avenue, London N10 2PS. Tel: 020 8444 3331. Website: www.angelproductions.co.uk.

Specialist UK producer of video-based training packs about Equality and Diversity at work. Subjects include harassment, disability, flexible work patterns and recruitment & selection.

Bully Online and the UK National Workplace Bullying Advice Line. Success Unlimited, Dept HE, P.O. Box 67, Didcot, Oxfordshire OX11 0YH. Tel: 01235 834548. Fax: 07000 785776. Email: timfield@successunlimited.co.uk. Internet: www.successunlimited.co.uk.

Free confidential advice and information on all aspects of workplace bullying. Also post-traumatic stress disorder (PTSD) and psychiatric injury. Major publications include: Workplace bullying information sheet and newsletter: Bully in sight: how to predict, resist, challenge and combat workplace bullying by Tim Field (send a cheque/PO for £14.85 made payable to 'Success Unlimited' to: Success Unlimited, at the address above); Post Traumatic Stress Disorder: the invisible injury by David Kinchin (send a cheque/PO for £15.00 made payable to 'Success Unlimited' to: Success Unlimited at the address above).

The Andrea Adams Trust. Maritime House, Basin Road North, Portslade, Brighton, East Sussex BN41 1WA. Tel: 01273 704900. Fax: 01273 704901. Email: aat@btinternet.com.

This is a professional body supported by membership and a registered charity. The Trust is a non-political, not-for-profit charity, operating as the focus for the complex problems caused by bullying behaviour in the workplace. The Trust is committed to raising awareness of the issue and providing support to victims of workplace bullying through a Helpline service and a factsheet. Through its consultancy arm – the Andrea Adams Consultancy – it provides a range of services to employers to reduce the incidence of workplace bullying including training, mediation, and bespoke consultancy services. Major publications include: 'Bullying at work – How to confront and overcome it'. Guides to 'Workplace Bullying – The Legal Position' and 'Workplace Bullying – International Research' (revised periodically).

The Domino Consultancy Limited. Field House, 19-23 Field Street, Shepshed, Leicestershire, LE12 9AL. Tel: +44 (0) 1509 821770. Fax: +44 (0) 1509 821774. Website: www.dominoconsultancy.co.uk/workshop.htm.

Specialists in Diversity and Equal Opportunities workshops.

The Dignity at Work Bill

This Bill was introduced in the House of Lords on 3 December 2001 and includes the following extracts.

1. Right to dignity at work

(1) Every employee shall have a right to dignity at work and if the terms of the contract under which a person is employed do not include that right they shall be deemed to include it.

(2) Subject to Section 5 of this Act, an employer commits a breach of the right to dignity at work of an employee if that employee suffers during his employment with the employer harassment or bullying or any act, omission or conduct which causes him to be alarmed or distressed including but not limited to any of the following:

(a) behaviour on more than one occasion which is offensive, abusive, malicious, insulting or intimidating;
(b) unjustified criticism on more than one occasion.

2. Victimisation

An employer commits a breach of the right to dignity at work of an employee if he treats that employee less favourably than he would treat other persons and does so by reason that the employee has:

(a) brought procedings under this Act against the employer or any other person;

(b) given evidence or information in connection with procedings brought by any person under this Act against the employer or any other person;

(c) otherwise done anything under or by reference to this Act in relation to the employer or any other person;

(d) alleged that the employer or any other person has committed an act which (whether or not the allegation so states) would give rise to a claim under this Act, or by reason that the employer knows or suspects that the employee has done or intends to do any of those things.

To view the entire Bill, visit:
www.parliament.the-stationery-office.co.uk/pa/ld200102/ldbills/031/2002031.htm

Further Reading

Men are from Mars, Women are from Venus, John Gray, HarperCollins

Assertiveness, C Beels, Management 2000 Books

Why Men Don't Listen and Women Can't Read Maps, Allan & Barbara Pease, Pease International

Turning Practical Communication into Business Power, B Katz, Management 2000 Books

Talking from Nine to Five, Deborah Tannen, Virago Press

The X and Y of Leadership, Liz Cook & Brian Rothwell, Industrial Society

How to Design and Deliver Equal Opportunities Training, Judith Taylor, Helen Garrett, Kogan Page

Index